HAZRAT AMIR KHUSRAU
OF DELHI

Other similar **INDIGO BOOKS** available (or to be published shortly) are.

SUFISM. ITS SAINTS AND SHRINES, John A. Subhan

HISTORY OF URDU LITERATURE, R. B. Saksena

THE MYSTICS OF ISLAM, Christian D. Larson

THE DARVISHES, OR ORIENTAL SPIRITUALISM, J. P. Brown

RUMI. POET AND MYSTIC, R. A. Nicholson

SUFISM. AN ACCOUNT OF THE MYSTICS IN ISLAM, A. J. Arberry

For getting information on our forthcoming books please write to us.

available from COSMO

ENCYCLOPAEDIA OF INDIAN MYSTICISM, in 12 volumes
***Edited by* Sadhu Santideva**

Now announcing the much awaited reference work...

THE MUSLIMS. ENCYCLOPAEDIA OF ISLAM
in 11 large volumes
Ed. Subodh Kapoor

Now available again ... New Edition ... established as the most authoritative reference book on Islam

DICTIONARY OF ISLAM,
Patric Hughes

HAZRAT AMIR KHUSRAU
OF DELHI

By
Mohammad Habib
C.B.E., B.A. (OXON.), M.L.C.
PROFESSOR OF HISTORY AND POLITICS,
MUSLIM UNIVERSITY, ALIGARH

INDIGO BOOKS

AN
INDIGO BOOK
PUBLISHED BY INDIGO BOOKS
Paperback division of
COSMO PUBLICATIONS,
24-B, Ansari Road, Darya Ganj,
New Delhi 110 002, India.

INDIGO BOOKS and
COSMO PUBLICATIONS
are wholly owned subsidiaries of
GENESIS PUBLISHING PVT. LTD.,
New Delhi, India

HAZRAT AMIR KHUSRAU OF DELHI

ISBN 81-292-0139-9

PRINTED AND BOUND IN INDIA

To

THE HON'BLE NAWAB

SIR MOHAMMAD MUZAMMILULLAH KHAN

K.C.I.E., O.B.E.,

(Rais-i Azam, Bhikampur, U.P.),

Vice-Chancellor, Aligarh Muslim University.

PREFACE

In a period of history which can boast of a splendid gallery of portraits, Amir Khusrau is one of the most attractive figures. I have not, in the present short work, tried to go into details, and my purpose has been primarily historical. My temperament as well as my training has prevented me from doing justice to the orthodox virtues of Khusrau's works—his hyperbolic praises, original figures of speech and hair-splitting distinctions. It is as a student of history that I have tried to approach him, and I humbly hope that, by relying entirely on contemporary authorities, I have done something to clear the way for the future biographer of Amir Khusrau.

My grateful thanks are due to Mr. Hamid A. Ali, I.C.S., for many helpful suggestions.

MOHAMMAD HABIB.

Muslim University, Aligarh.

April 10th, 1927.

CONTENTS

CHAPTER I

LIFE OF AMIR KHUSRAU

"There were poets in the reign of Sultan Alauddin Khilji," Ziauddin Barni remarks in his famous *Tarikh-i Feroz Shahi,* "such as had never existed before and have never appeared since. The incomparable Amir Khusrau stands unequalled for the volume of his writings and the originality of his ideals; for, while other great masters of prose and verse have excelled in one or two branches, Amir Khusrau was conspicuous in every department of letters. A man with such mastery over all the forms of poetry has never existed in the past and may perhaps not come into existence before the Day of Judgment. And in addition to his wit, talent and learning, he was an advanced mystic.[(1)] He fasted every day and passed

---

(1) A detailed biography of Amir Khusrau cannot be attempted here, and I must refer the more inquisitive reader to the sources of information available. The most comprehensive modern account is to be found in Maulana Shibli Nomani's *Shi'rul Ajam* (Volume II, pages 107-195), the greatest achievement of Indo-Muslim scholarship in these later days. The historical part of Maulana Shibli's chapter, however, suffers from an uncritical reliance on secondary authorities. Amir Khusrau has given a short biography of himself in the Introduction to his *Gharratul Kamal,* and

most of his time in reading the *Quran*, and in obligatory and supererogatory prayers. He was one of the chief disciples of Shaikh Nizamuddin Aulia; and a disciple with a firmer faith in his master I have never seen. Of love and affection, too, he had his full share, and he was a man of ecstasy and rapture. He excelled in the playing and composition of music. Almighty God had bestowed on him all the qualities that appertain to an artistic and cultured mind. He was, in fact, a wonderful being, a strange phenomenon for these later times. I have lived for years on terms of friendship with him and the mystic-poet, Amir Hasan; they did not feel happy without my company, nor did I without theirs. Through me an intimacy sprang up between these two masters, and they began to frequent each other's houses."

An eminent modern critic fully agrees with Barni's tribute to his friend. "No person of such comprehensive ability," Maulana Shibli remarks in the

---

speaks of himself again and again in his other works. The most reliable of contemporary accounts is Ziauddin Barni's *Tarikh-i Feroz Shahi,* which, so far as I can make out, was not utilised by Maulana Shibli. A somewhat later work, the *Siyarul Aulia* (Chapter V) of Amir Khurd, gives a short account of Khusrau based on what the author had heard from his father, who knew the poet personally. Contemporary accounts, if carefully sifted, will yield sufficient material for a reliable biography, but later writers, unfortunately, have saved themselves from all trouble by giving credence to many baseless stories. Abdul Qadir Badauni (*Muntakhibut Tawarikh,* Volume I) was content to put down whatever he had come across in the course of his desultory reading. Daulat Shah's notice of Khusrau in the *Tazkiratush Shu'ara* (Professor Browne's edition, pages 238-247) is an extreme example of historical confusion and uncritical praise. Ferishta, on the whole, adheres carefully to his authorities.

Shi'rul Ajam, "has been born in India during the last six hundred years, and even the fertile soil of Persia has produced only three or four persons of such varied accomplishments in a thousand years. To take poetry alone, Khusrau's mastery over all its forms is marvellous. Firdausi, Sa'di, Anwari, Hafiz, 'Urfi and Naziri are kings in the realm of verse, but the sway of each of them was confined to one section of it only. Firdausi could not advance beyond the *masnavi,* Sadi could not write *qasidas,* Anwari had no power over the *ghazal* or the *masnavi,* while Hafiz, 'Urfi and Naziri were unable to step outside the circle of the *ghazal.* But Khusrau's comprehensive genius takes the *ghazal* as well as the *masnavi, qasida,* and *rubai* within its all-embracing fold, together with the minor departments of versification such as *mustazad, sana-'i* and *bada-'i.*(2) For sheer quantity no one can equal him. Firdausi's couplets amount to about seventy thousand, Saib has been responsible for over a hundred thousand, but Amir Khusrau's couplets number several *lacs.* In some *tazkirahs* (biographies of poets) the number is said to be between three and four lacs. But there is, probably, a misunderstanding here. Khusrau uses the word *bait,* and *bait,* in the terminology of the earlier writers, means not a couplet but a single line.

"In addition to this, Auhadi remarks in the *Tazkira-i Urfat* that Khusrau's work in *Brij Bhasha*

---

(2) For an explanation of the various forms of Persian verse here mentioned, see Prof. Browne's *Literary History of Persia,* Vol. II.

(Hindi) was as extensive as his work in Persian; if this be true, it is to be greatly regretted that those compositions should have been entirely lost.(3) As a linguist, our author had Persian and Turkish for his mother tongues,(4) while his command over Arabic was as great as that of its greatest men of letters. He was a scholar of Sanskrit also. 'I have obtained some knowledge of it,' he modestly confesses in the

---

(3) This is highly improbable. A number of Khusrau's Hindi compositions still survive, but the volume of his work in Hindi could not have been very large. What swelled his Persian work to its abnormal extent was the necessity of writing for his bread. In Hindi that incentive was wanting, and he wrote for pleasure only.

(4) This is only partially true. Amir Khusrau was born in India, and his mother was of Indian birth. It appears from the social conditions of the time that Hindi and Persian were almost equally the mother tongues of most Indian Mussalmans of the middle class. Much, of course, depended on the individual family. Amongst newly settled families, like those of Amir Khusrau, the predominance was in favour of Persian. No reader of his works can doubt that the Persian language was the natural vehicle of Khusrau's thought; he lived in it as a fish lives in water. With the older families and the converts from Hinduism it was different. They had great facilities for learning Persian, which was the language of polite society, but none the less it was acquired with effort. Khusrau's friend, Barni, is a good example. Barni and Khusrau both mixed Hindi with Persian, but the latter did it consciously, while passage after passage of the *Tarikh-i Ferozi* seems to be a painful translation from Hindi into Persian. Turkish never became popular with the *literati* of India, though most of the royal dynasties, as well as middle-class Muslim immigrants, belonged to the Turkish race. Turkish titles and technical terms survived to a much later date, specially in the army, but knowledge of the language was slowly decreasing. Khusrau's works show an acquaintance with Turkish, but he never seems to have written in that language, possibly because the audience would have been extremely limited. The bulk of the population, whether Hindu or Muslim, spoke and knew no other language but Hindi.

Nuh Sipahr. He was a prose writer as well, and wrote the *'Ijaz-i Khusravi*, a work in three (? five) volumes, on the principles of prose composition; and though, unfortunately, most of it is devoted to figures of speech, no reader of the book will deny the inventive genius of the author. Khusrau was an accomplished musician, and no one after him has been able to obtain the title of *Naik*.(5) Devoted as he was to these occupations, Khusrau was at heart a mystic, who never cared to turn his eyes from the spiritual to the material world. It is strange how he managed to find time for all his work. He was in service from the beginning of his career and had to be present in the courts (of *amirs* and kings) from morning till sunset, and poetry was not the only duty they required of him.(6)

---

(5) Khusrau's eminence as a musician is generally admitted. "I am a master of music as well as of poetry," he says in a *qita* quoted by Daulat Shah, "I have written three volumes of poetry and my musical compositions would also amount to three volumes, if they could be reduced to writing." Maulana Shibli quotes from the *Rag Darpan*, a Persian translation of *Manik Sohal* made in the reign of Aurangzeb, a number of *rags* and *raginis*, which Khusrau is said to have invented. The same later authority is responsible for the following anecdote. Naik Gopal was a musician of all-India fame in the time of Alauddin Khilji. He had sixteen hundred disciples who used to carry about his litter on their shoulders. Invited to the court of the Khilji Emperor, Gopal gave demonstrations of his *rags* at six different sittings, during which Khusrau was hiding under the throne. At the seventh sitting Khusrau confronted Gopal and invited him to show his powers. He claimed that all Gopal's *rags* had been previously invented by him, and his imitation was so perfect as to bewilder the Hindu master.

(6) *Khan, malik* and *amir* were official titles during the middle ages, and indicated the status of the officer. Generally speaking, an *amir* meant an officer in command of 100 men,

"The Creator Himself may be well proud of such a creation."

The man of letters, of whom contemporaries as well as posterity have had such a high opinion, came from a family of respectable Turkish immigrants. Among the many unhappy people, whom Chengiz Khan's invasion of Central Asia drove out of their homes as refugees to India, was the Turkish tribe of Lachin, whose original habitation seems to have been the town of Takash in the province of Mawaraun Nahr (Trans-Oxonia). Sultan Shamsuddin I-ltutmish warmly welcomed the immigrants.(7) Khusrau's father, Saifuddin, was one of the leaders of the Lachin Turks, and his mother was the daughter of 'Imadul Mulk, Balban's Minister of War (*arz-i mumalik*). The poet was born in the town of Patiali in 652 A.H. (1254 A.D.).(8) The new-born child, wrapped in a cloth, was taken to a mystic who had settled in the

---

a *malik* of 1,000, and a *khan* of 10,000 men, though in practice this decimal system, borrowed from the military organisation of the Turks, was not strictly followed. Civil and military duties were combined; consequently, a command in the army meant a corresponding status in the civil administration and *vice versa*. The word *amir*, nevertheless, was used as a generic term to include all government officers, however high their designation.

(7) *Daulat Shah*. The *Shi'rul Ajam*, relying on the *Baharistan Sukhan*, accuses Daulat Shah of bringing the Lachins into India in the reign of Mohammad Tughlaq. This is, however, a mistake. Daulat Shah says Shamsuddin Mohammad, meaning the Emperor I-ltutmish.

(8) So I conclude from the *Qiranus Sa'dain*, which was completed in 688 A.H. when, the author says, he was thirty-six years of age. The *Shi'rul Ajam* says 605 A.H., an obvious mistake.

neighbourhood. "Amir Lachin," the mystic exclaimed, "you have brought to me one who will go two steps beyond Khaqani."(9) Khusrau's father died while he was only seven, but the family was in affluent circumstances and his education was well attended to. His later works display an extensive and accurate knowledge of the science and philosophy of his day, but the irrepressible bent of his genius lay in the direction of poetry. He began writing verses from his boyhood, and by the time he had reached his twentieth year, his occupation in life was permanently settled.

Men of poetic genius have often been cursed with an irascible temperament that keeps them aloof from a humdrum world, in which a certain malleability of character is the first condition of success. But Amir Khusrau did not belong to that unhappy type which, perhaps, includes the greatest thinkers of east and west. He was too human to be a mere poet. Every inch an artist, he was none the less a shrewd man of affairs. He could wield the sword as well as the pen, and his capacity for enjoying the passing hour prevented his life from being cursed, or blessed, with that exclusive devotion to their art, from which poets less happily circumstanced have sought a consolation for all earthly failures. For three quarters of a century Delhi had been the capital of India, and many causes had combined to raise it to the magnitude of a second Baghdad. Hither fled the nobles, scholars and politicians whom the Mongol conquest of

(9) *Siyarul Aulia.* The incident is related by Amir Khurd on the authority of his father.

Muslim Asia had driven for refuge to a foreign, but not inhospitable, land. Here also flocked all the worst and best elements of Indian society—astrologers, artisans, musicians, assassins, *thugs,* sharpers and *budmashes* of every variety and kind. Delhi became the home of all arts, fine and coarse, and opened a door to clever and talented men. In the suburbs and slums of the great capital the pimps, prostitutes and gamblers of Hindustan collected together to ply their abominable trades; and along with them, as a Heaven-sent antidote, came innumerable mystics and preachers, whose desperate efforts could barely prevent the Capital from rushing headlong, like an avalanche, into the open jaws of Hell. In this city of sunshine and shadow Amir Khusrau's genius found a natural home. It had much to teach him, and he was eager to learn. He saw Delhi in all her phases—the eloquence of her preachers, the ecstatic discourses of her mystics and the alluring blandishments of her dancing-girls—and when he took up his pen to write, he found his heart throbbing with the deepest human emotions. "I have gathered the fruits of every tree," Shaikh Sa'di of Shiraz had said, and Khusrau, who prided himself on having poured the 'wine of Shiraz into his goblet,' followed the footsteps of his distinguished predecessor,(10) and investigated life in all its manifold phases from the Imperial Palace to the working class slum, from the monastery to the brothel. Artificial and conventional as are many

(10) *"Khusravi sarmast andar saghar-i ma'ni birikht*
"Shira as khumkhang-i masti ki dar Shiraz bud."
See also *'Ijaz-i Khusravi,* Vol. V.

of Khusrau's works, the defect was due to the tradition of the age, not to the author's ignorance of the realities of life.

Still bread had to be earned. A reckless liberality, that took no thought of the morrow, was the one redeeming virtue of the Turkish nobility of the day, and Khusrau was as large-hearted as any of them. "Share with those who need whatever it pleases the Lord to bestow on thee," is his advice to his son in the *Aina-i Sikandari,* "Remove the crust of selfishness from thy heart and the look of sourness from thy brow. Give with a pleasant face whatever thou hast, and thy liberality will be twice blessed. Shower thy gifts on all and attach them to thyself, like the lion who entertains the beasts of the forest on the game it kills—not like the cat that withdraws into a corner whenever it has found a morsel to eat. Yes, and let strangers partake of thy liberality, for every silly ass can be generous to his wife and children. The man whose kindness extends to his family only is really selfish."(11) To a person of such views even a modest competence was galling, and Khusrau had no intention of remaining poor. Like most men of genius, he felt disgusted at the idea of becoming rich through slow and persistent labour, and selected the only profession that, in his day, combined the minimum of labour with the maximum of profit, and yet did not take him too far from what he conceived to be his destined mission in life. He became a courtier. The statesmen of the middle ages patronised

---

(11) Aligarh edition, pages 38 and 46.

poets as their modern successors patronise the printing press. The panegyrics of the poet created a public opinion in favour of his patron and passed his name from mouth to mouth, and if he was wise and discriminating in his selection, a fraction of the poet's immortality also fell to his share. Khusrau, on his part, was wonderfully suited to such a career. He wrote *qasidas* and *ghazals* with the same rapidity as our modern journalists write their daily editorials. He could accommodate himself to the requirements of every company. His personality was attractive, his wit brilliant and his conversation charming. In the stormy political atmosphere of the day, such a path, no doubt, had its dangers, but Khusrau was as discreet as he was pushing and never climbed to dizzy heights. It was difficult to remain a courtier without becoming a politician, but Khusrau never involved himself in the political ventures of his patrons. He maintained with them relations of good fellowship and pure business. He sang their praises because he was paid for doing so, and he insisted on being paid handsomely. For half a century, the iridescent bubbles passed before his admiring eyes, and he praised them in hyperbolic terms. But he forgot the bubble the moment it had burst. The horizon always revealed a rising star, and to that star the poet made his way with his pilgrim's staff and his mellifluous verse. It is not given to any mortal to be perfectly happy, but Amir Khusrau's career was one Epicurus himself would have envied and approved.

Khusrau's first patron, Alauddin Mohammad Kushil Khan, generally known as *Malik Chajju,* whose service he seems to have entered in 1277 A.D., was the nephew and *Amir-i Hajib* (Grand Chamberlain) of the Emperor Ghiasuddin Balban.(12) "I have often heard from reliable persons, specially from Amir Khusrau," Barni notes in his history, "that Malik Alauddin Kushil Khan's equal in large-heartedness and generosity, in shooting, hunting and playing the ball (13) has never been born." Malik Chajju, certainly, obtained a reputation which was as extensive as it was transitory. The famous Halaku sent him a dagger and offered him the governorship of one half of Iraq, if he cared to go thither; and the Emperor Balban, a sombre and close-fisted man, is said to have resented his nephew's extraordinary liberality.(14) Not a little of this reputation was due to Chajju's treatment of poets. On his appointment to the governorship of Karra (Allahabad), he gave away all the horses in his stable to a poet, Khwaja Shams Mo'in, for reciting a sonorous *qasida,* and distributed ten thousand *tankas* amongst the musicians. At other times, Barni would have us believe, Chajju's fits of generosity were so strong that he gave all his property to the objects of his favour and kept nothing for himself excepting the cloak that covered his body. Like other poets, Khusrau also

---

(12) Maulana Shibli takes some pains to show that Malik Chajju and Kushil Khan indicate the same person. A reader of Barni will have no doubt about it. Chajju was a mere nickname, while his father's title of Kushil Khan was bestowed on him by the Emperor Balban after his father's death.

(13) *i.e., chaugan,* the mediæval polo.

(14) *Tarikh-i Ferozi,* B. R. A. S. text, pages 113 and 114.

basked in the warmth of the sun and rapidly made his mark. His most famous *qasida* (panegyric) on Malik Chajju is a typical example of oriental hyperbolism:—

The radiant glow of amber-coloured dawn
Had just dispelled the darkness of the night;
The yellow crescent with its curving horns
And jaundiced looks was sinking out of sight.
I asked the morn: " Where is thy promised sun?"
And Chajju's face shone with its rising light.

I turned next to the starry heaven and asked:
" Say what supports thy planets in their flight?"
It smiled at my vain question and displayed
The Malik's arms that held them all upright.(15)

A trifling incident, however, alienated Malik Chajju's heart from the poet after the latter had served him for two years. Balban's second son, Nasiruddin Bughra Khan, was once present at a party of Malik Chajju, and, being pleased with some verses of Khusrau, presented him with a basin of silver coins. Chajju was annoyed at the poet's accepting the gift. Khusrau tried again and again to win back his patron's favour. But it was of no avail, and he finally transferred his services to Bughra Khan, then

(15) " *Subh chun az sui mashriq ru namud, sahn mina rauza-i minu namud.*" (Niwal Kishore edition, pages 32 and 33.)

governor of Samana. He had not been long with his new patron when Tughril, the governor of Lakhnauti, rebelled, and the Emperor marched against him in person. The unambitious and ineffectual Bughra Khan was compelled to accompany his father and took the poet along with him. The rebels were subdued, and, after a series of vindictive punishments, that sent a shudder through the length and breadth of Hindustan, Balban appointed Bughra Khan governor of the conquered province. Khusrau seems to have lingered on at Lakhnauti after the Emperor's return, but the atmosphere of an eastern provincial town was uncongenial to his temperament. He took leave of his master and came back to Delhi, where chance brought him into contact with the most cultured and most generous of his patrons, the Emperor's eldest son, Sultan Mohammad, known to later generations as the *Khan-i Shahid* ("Martyr Prince").

Sultan Mohammad was an ideal prince according to the standard of the age. He was brave, polite, urbane. He never used foul language and seldom drank to excess. No one could preside better at a meeting of government officers, mystics or poets; he sat for hours at a stretch without showing the slightest weariness by a movement of his limbs. He appreciated poetry and patronised art. His anthology (*biaz*) of Persian verse contained about thirty thousand couplets and was praised by eminent critics for its discriminating selection and extensive knowledge.(16) The Emperor entrusted to the son he

(16) "This *biaz* was a wonderful manuscript. After the prince's death, Sultan Balban gave it to his ink-bearer,

loved more than his own life the most difficult duty of the day—the wardenship of the frontier marches. For over half a century the Mongol storm had been lowering over the western horizon and constantly threatened to burst. A panic used to seize the towns and villages of India at the very name of the invaders, who 'came like ants and locusts' and left a desolate wilderness behind them wherever they went. The fall of Delhi seemed only a question of time, for no one had the courage to face the conquering barbarian. Balban's stout-hearted cousin, the valiant Sher Khan, had done yeoman service to the Empire by his vigilant protection of the Punjab. But early in his reign Balban had poisoned his cousin from jealousy, and the frontier was left unprotected. Sultan Mohammad, on succeeding to Sher Khan's office, won the golden opinion of all people. His court at Multan became famous throughout the Persian-reading world. "The *majlis* of Sultan Mohammad was composed of learned scholars and artists; his courtiers used to read the *Shah Namah,* the *Diwans* of Sana'i and Khaqani and the *Khamsah* of Nizami and discussed the merits of various poets before him." On coming to Delhi (1280 A.D.) with the revenues of the provinces of the Punjab and Sindh, Sultan Mohammad met Amir Khusrau and took him to Multan. "For five years Amir Khusrau and Amir Hasan were in his service at Multan..........and with the keen judgment that he

---

Amir Ali, and from him it came into the hands of Amir Khusrau." (*Shi'rul Ajam.*) A *biaz* is a manuscript collection of poems which Indians are even now very fond of compiling.

had, the prince at once recognised their merit, placed them above his other courtiers, paid them higher salaries and presented them with better robes of honour." The ambitious prince even attempted to bring a greater poet than Amir Khusrau to his provincial capital. Twice he sent messengers to Shaikh Sa'di of Shiraz with the expenses of the journey and offered to build and endow a monastery for the Shaikh at Multan. But Sa'di excused himself on the ground of old age and sent prince *ghazals* written with his own hand.(17)

"But suddenly a bolt fell from the blue; the Day of Doom was enacted on earth, and the company of friends was dispersed like rose-petals scattered by the autumnal winds that desolate the garden."(18) As if in punishment for his father's murder of Sher Khan, Sultan Mohammad lost his life in resisting a Mongol raid. In 687 A.H. (1285 A.D.) a Mongol general, named I-tmar, invaded the Punjab with thirty thousand men, and Sultan Mohammad marched against him. But through a strange error, the prince had read 'three thousand' instead of 'thirty thousand' in the message sent to him, and on coming face to face with the enemy near Lahore, he discovered that the small force he had brought was utterly insufficient to take the field. He fortified himself in a village on the eastern bank of the Ravi and was waiting for

---

(17) According to Badauni, Shaikh Sa'di further recommended Amir Khusrau to the prince's favour and praised him beyond limits. This statement, whether false or true, is not found in Barni.

(18) Khusrau's *Elegy,* quoted by Badauni.

reinforcements, when the Mongols surprised him by crossing the river at midday and breaking into his camp. Sultan Mohammad was forced to give battle; but, in spite of all his courage, the field was irretrievably lost, and at sunset the prince himself was mortally wounded by an arrow. Delhi and Multan mourned the news. The old Sultan was crushed. All day he sat in the court and attended to the business of the government, but at night he gave way to lamentation and tears. Every one could see that his end, too, was not far off.

Amir Khusrau was not only a courtier but also an officer in the army. He had accompanied his master and was captured by the Mongols. "The Muslim martyrs dyed the desert with their blood," he says,(19) "while the Muslim captives had their necks tied together like so many flowers into garlands. I was also taken prisoner, and from fear that they would shed my blood, not a drop of blood remained in my veins. I ran about like water, here and there, with innumerable blisters on my feet like bubbles on the surface of a stream. My tongue was parched and dry from excessive thirst and my stomach seemed to have collapsed for want of food. They (took away my clothes from me and) left me nude like a leafless tree in winter or a flower that has been much lacerated by thorns. My Mongol captor sat on a horse like a lion bestriding the spur of a mountain; a

---

(19) In a *qasida* quoted by Badauni (B. R. A. S. text, pages 151-154). The curious incident by which he acquired his freedom is described in the *Dawal Rani* (Aligarh edition, page 36).

disgusting stench came out of his mouth and his armpits, and on his chin there grew, like a hyacinth, a tuft as of pubic hair. If through weakness I lagged a little behind, he would threaten me sometimes with his frying-pan and sometimes with his spear. I sighed and thought that release from such a situation was quite impossible. But, thank God, I did regain my freedom without my breast having been pierced by an arrow or my body cut into two by the sword." On reaching a stream, probably the Ravi, the thirsty Mongol and his no less thirsty horse plunged into the water, drank their fill and almost instantly yielded up the ghost. The cautious Khusrau moistened his lips, which brought some relief to his palpitating heart, and fled.[20] At Delhi he found his mother broken by anxiety and suspense, and gave expression to the emotions of the hour in an elegy on the martyred prince. The graphic touches of an eye-witness, combined with the grief of one who had personally suffered the loss of a munificent patron, secured it an immediate popularity. For over a month Khusrau's verses were recited before weeping faces in court and camp. It is, in fact, an inimitable piece of art. The thrill of horror that

---

(20) Maulana Shibli says that Khusrau was taken a prisoner to Balkh. This is incorrect. His captivity and release are events of a single day. The battle began at noon and ended at sunset. It was a hot April day and the excessive thirst to which Khusrau refers is quite intelligible. The evening must have been far advanced when the Ravi was reached, and the increasing darkness made the poet's escape easier. Being an officer, he was accorded a differential treatment and kept apart for the sake of ransom from those who were 'tied into garlands by the neck.'

swept over the country, the superb self-confidence of the prince on his march from Multan, the sudden rush of the Mongols, the desperate stand of the Indian army in the scorching heat and the ineffectual attempts of the remnant to escape are described in a melodious verse of sustained and indescribable sadness. Hitherto Khusrau's Persian verses had been only current among the educated; the elegy made his name familiar to the man in the street.(21)

For some time after the sad event Amir Khusrau remained at Patiali with his adored mother. Events at Delhi were taking an unfortunate turn. Balban had been succeeded by his grandson, Muizzuddin Kai-Kabad, a young man of eighteen, who started on a career of reckless dissipation; and the affairs of the state were left in the hands of the Minister, Nizamuddin, a grasping politician about whom his own uncle, Fakhruddin, the *Kotwal* of Delhi, declared that 'he had not the courage to throw a stone at a jackal or to thrash a grocer with an onion-leaf.' Everything was falling into disorder, and men of discernment could see the signs of a coming revolution. The politicians round the young Emperor bore no love to the memory of Sultan Mohammad, whose son, Kai-Khusrau, they had put to death. It was impossible for the poet to gain a footing at the Imperial Court while Nizamuddin was in power, and he had no alternative but to seek safety in a provincial

---

(21) Amir Khusrau's elegy is transcribed by Badauni from the *Gharratul Kamal*. He also copies a prose elegy by Amir Hasan.

capital.(22) Amir Ali Sarjandar, generally known as Hatim Khan, was one of the most senior members of the official hierarchy, and his patronage seemed an anchor of safety in the dangerous days ahead.(23) Amir Ali had started his career as a freedman of the Emperor Balban, but had risen to be one of the greatest persons in the land. He had a reputation for generosity. "Even to beggars, who wander from door to door, he gave *tankas* of gold and silver: the name of *jital* never came to his lips."(24) Khusrau, like others, also paid many tributes to Hatim Khan's munificience:—

"Thou art generous like the Khan," I told the sea.
"Oh No! Oh No!" its trembling soul replied,
"My stingy waves cast off but worthless weeds;
He scatters rubies in his generous pride."

The poet was already in Hatim Khan's service when the latter was appointed governor of Oudh. But after staying there for two years, Khusrau once

---

(22) Barni says that Sultan Mohammad and Fakhruddin, the *Kotwal*, had quarrelled over a woman. It was owing to Fakhruddin that Balban's will in favour of Kai-Khusrau was ignored and Kai-Kabad was placed on the throne. The poet himself was in no danger of persecution, but his retreat to Patiali, and later on to Oudh, was probably due to the dislike Nizamuddin had for him.

(23) *Sarjandar* meant the 'Commander of the Imperial Bodyguard.' He is called *Khan-i Jahan* in the *Shi'rul Ajam*, and Khusrau refers to him under that designation in the *Qiranus Sa'dain*.

(24) *Tanka* was the gold and silver coin of the day; *Jital* was the copper coin. According to Barni, Khusrau also wrote a poem, the *Asp Namah*, in Hatim Khan's praise.

more began to long for Delhi. His mother was anxious to see him, and Nizamuddin had fallen. Hatim Khan cordially permitted him to leave and presented him with two platefuls of gold coins for the expenses of the journey. Khusrau had not been two days in Delhi when a messenger of Muizzuddin Kai-Kabad came to invite him to the Imperial Court.(25) The poet kissed the ground and recited a *qasida;* the Emperor presented him with a waist-band and two purses of gold and asked him to write an account of his (Kai-Kabad's) meeting with his father, Bughra Khan. Khusrau was enrolled among the chief courtiers and sat down to compose his first *masnavi,* the *Qiranus Sa'dain,* which was completed after six months of continuous labour in Shawwal, 688 A.H. (October, 1289). But while the poet was busy over his *masnavi,* the Emperor rapidly went from bad to worse, and the dissipated habits, which he lacked strength to overcome, confined him to bed with a mortal malady at the young age of twenty-two. With him also fell the Turkish bureaucracy, which had monopolised all political power in the state from the time of Shahabuddin Ghori. Amir Khusrau had many friends among the Turkish nobles, but he looked with supreme unconcern at their fall. It was his principle to swim with the current, not against it.

The new Emperor, Sultan Jalaluddin Khilji, was an old admirer of Amir Khusrau. Many years previously Jalaluddin had conferred on Khusrau the military command of his father, Amir Lachin, a post that

---

(25) *Qiranus Sa'dain* (Aligarh edition, pages 221-230).

brought the poet about twelve hundred *tankas* a year with the title of *amir.* On his accession to the throne, Jalaluddin raised Khusrau to the highest status he was ever destined to reach. "He was assigned the office of 'Keeper of the Royal *Quran*' and became the chief courtier.(26) The Sultan presented him with the same robe of honour and white waist-band as were given to the greatest *maliks* of the land." Jalaluddin, though an old man of seventy, loved the charms of cultured society. His own verses were of no very high order, but his critical taste was superior to his creative power.(27) He had collected at his Court the best musicians, singers and dancing-girls that could be found in the country "and his pleasure-parties were such as can only be seen in dreams. While the *saqis* invited the company to drink and the musicians played and the dancing-girls performed, the recitation of Khusrau's *ghazals* restored the weary-hearted to life and transported the emotional to paradise." Apart from the *ghazals* and *qasidas* he wrote for the Sultan's parties, Khusrau also presented his master with the *Miftahul Futuh,* a versified history of his campaigns. Unfortunately, two of Khusrau's former patrons, Malik Chajju and Hatim Khan, rebelled against the Khilji Emperor, but the poet made a right-about turn

(26) The duties of a courtier (*nadim*) were kept quite distinct from those of a minister. He was required to entertain the Sultan's leisure hours but had nothing to do with the administration of the kingdom or matters of high policy. The office brought more profit than dignity or power.

(27) Two of the Sultan's quatrains are given by Badauni.

and congratulated the Sultan on his victory over the rebels. He was destined soon to swallow and digest a more bitter pill.

On the 16th of Ramzan, 695 A.H. (14th July, 1296 A.D.) the Emperor's nephew and son-in-law, Malik Alauddin Khilji, had his uncle assassinated by the side of the Ganges near Karra (Allahabad). It is one of the most atrocious murders that history records. Jalaluddin had brought up his nephew with the affection of a father and had condescended to visit his camp unaccompanied by his army. "Ungrateful Alauddin! What hast thou planned?" he cried as the assassin, Ikhtiaruddin Hud, ran after him and cut off his head, while his lips were repeating the oath of affirmation.(28) The new Emperor did not think it wise to offer any justification for the murder to which he owed his throne; he closed the mouths of his critics with gold and made his government firm and secure through his administrative and economic reforms. Alauddin's accession was followed by a veritable reign of terror; everything was cast into the furnace and moulded anew in consonance with the revolutionary Emperor's fervent imagination. Like others Khusrau also brought his offerings before 'the picture of fire.' Storms of righteous indignation may have swept across his soul at the outrageous murder of his patron, but not the humblest word of protest ever came to his

---

(28) "There is no God but *Allah* and Mohammad is His Prophet." The incident is described by Barni in detail.

lips.[29] His position as poet-laureate was quite secure; no one questioned his pre-eminence, and Alauddin accepted the poet along with the other furniture and decorations of his predecessor's Court. The Emperor was far from being an educated or cultured man, and Barni accuses him of not recognising the poet's worth. "If a poet like Amir Khusrau had lived in the time of Mahmud or Sanjar, those monarchs would have bestowed territories and governorships on him and raised him to high dignity and office. But Alauddin paid no regard to the honour due to such a poet and was content to give him his one thousand *tankas.*"[30] The Khilji statesman was, no doubt, too experienced in mundane affairs to turn the governorships of the Empire into playthings for wits and poets. He was feverishly busy in organising every department of the economic life of the people, and it is not to be wondered at that he was somewhat ungenerous to a class, which, from his point of view, appeared singularly unproductive. Still, judging from Khusrau's tributes to the Emperor's munificence, the poet's labour obviously did not go unrewarded. There was also another reason for Khusrau's rhyme. For the first time in his career he had come face to face with a statesman who really deserved his praise. Malik Chajju and Bughra Khan, Jalaluddin and Sultan

---

(29) In the *Khazainul Futuh* as well as the *Dawal Rani* Khusrau simply refrains from making any reference to Jalaluddin's assassination. This was, doubtless, in accordance with Alauddin's wish, who desired the incident to be forgotten.

(30) Twelve hundred would be more accurate. This was Khusrau's salary as a government officer.

Mohammad were men of ordinary stature and owed their prominence to accident or birth. With Alauddin, a real hero appeared on the stage; and Amir Khusrau, with a true insight into the poet's art, cast off hyperbole for reality and sang as he had never sung before. There is something singularly gracious and becoming in the *qasidas* in which the greatest of our mediæval poets has paid his tribute to the greatest of our mediæval Emperors.

The twenty years of Alauddin's reign coincided with the most productive period of Khusrau's life. He was as absorbed in his poetry as the Emperor was in his reforms, and his speed was surprising. In three years 698-700 A.H. (1298-1300 A.D.) he completed his five romantic *masnavis*—*Matla'ul Anwar, Shirin Khusrau, Majnun Laila, Aina-i Sikandari* and *Hasht Bihisht*—which are collectively known as the *Panj Ganj*. All these *masnavis* were dedicated to Shaikh Nizamuddin Aulia and presented to Sultan Alauddin. While he was writing his third volume, the *Majnun Laila,* he lost his much-loved mother and his younger brother. "This year, 697 A.H.," he says, "two stars have disappeared from my firmament; my mother and brother have both departed. Where are you, O mother mine, that I cannot see you? Have mercy on my tears and come smiling out of your grave! In days gone by I was as insolent as you were loving, and now that I am ashamed of my conduct, how can I ask your forgiveness? While a man is blessed with prosperity, he does not recognise its value, and when that blessing has departed, rubbing hands in anxiety does not bring it back again! Your advice was the support of my life when your lips could speak—and your silence inspires me still!......... And with you is gone Qutlugh, your son and my brother. He had completed all the stages of the warrior's training and so fortune gave him the title of *Hisam* (sword). He charged valiantly, like my father, on the field of battle; he never lagged behind like me, a man with a broken sword. But now, without comrades and without friends, how are you faring in your lonesome grave? Oh, let me see you; do not trurn away your face. Wake up, wake up! You have slept too long. Or, if you are too pure for my physical eye to perceive, at least come to me in my dreams."(31) In spite of this bereavement, Khusrau brought the series to a conclusion. "Thank God!" he says gratefully at the end of the *Hasht Bihisht*, "He has thrown so many gems into my hands from the unseen treasure that I have filled my five treasure houses (*Panj Ganj*) with them in three years. Transitory as is my life, I need have no anxiety now that the edifice is complete."

The five romantic *masnavis* would have satisfied a poet less ambitious and worn out one less virile. But Khusrau's energies never slackened. As if afraid that his critics would dismiss him merely as a poet, he turned to prose and brought out two works of different lengths. The first, *Khazainul Futuh*, is a thin volume on the history of Alauddin's wars; the second, *'Ijaz-i*

---

(31) *Majnun Laila* (Aligarh edition, pages 160-165).

Khusravi, is a long work in five volumes on figures of speech. Towards the end of Alauddin's reign came the second and best of Khusrau's historical *masnavis*, the *Dawal Rani Khizr Khan*, which the course of events brought to a tragic conclusion.

No biographer of Amir Khusrau can afford to ignore the influence exercised on him by Shaikh Nizamuddin Aulia.[32] Different as were their characters and temperaments, their admiration for each other was genuine and sincere. The course of their early lives had been utterly dissimilar. Shaikh Nizamuddin's paternal grandfather, Khwaja Syed Ali, had emigrated from Bokhara and settled in Badaun, where the Shaikh was born in 1238 A.D. While he was yet a child, his father, Syed Ahmad, fell ill and his mother, Bibi Zulaikha, dreamt that a voice was asking her to choose between her husband and her son. With the eternal instinct of the Indian mother, Bibi Zulaikha preferred to save her son, and as destiny would have it, Syed Ahmed died soon after. Bibi Zulaikha was a lady of fervent piety, and her character left a deep impression on the son, whom she adored and managed to educate in conditions of appalling poverty. Mother and son had no means of livelihood except what their neighbours brought to them unasked, and their maid-servant ran away from the starving household. Nevertheless, the Shaikh, who was

---

(32) Popular usage nowadays divides Indian Mussalmans into *Syeds, Moghuls, Pathans* and a fourth, extensive and nondescript class, designated *Shaikhs*. In mediæval India, however, a *Shaikh* meant an eminent mystic or saint. I have used the term in its mediæval significance.

remarkable for his diligence, learnt all that Badaun had to teach, and, at the age of sixteen, went with his mother and sister to complete his studies at Delhi. The great capital was then full of scholars and men of learning; education was practically free; and a student so intelligent as the Shaikh had access to the best teachers. His principal tutor, Maulana Kamal-uddin Zahid, was distinguished by a remarkable independence of character. Sultan Ghiasuddin Balban, having heard of Maulana Zahid's piety, invited him to the Court and offered him the post of Head Imam. "Our prayer is all that is left to us," the Maulana replied, "Does the Sultan wish to seize that also?" Balban was struck dumb, and, after offering a brief apology, allowed the Maulana to depart. From such a scholar Shaikh Nizamuddin obtained his final certificate at the age of twenty and, perhaps, also imbibed that indifference towards men of wordly grandeur that distinguished him throughout his life.

Though he had hitherto followed the normal course of studies, the Shaikh's mind was already inclined towards mysticism, and he often told his comrades that he would not for long remain in the atmosphere of their literary discussions. At the age of twelve he had heard a *qawwal* (33) praise the piety of Shaikh Farid Ganj Shakar of Ajodhan; ever since then he had developed an extraordinary reverence for that saint and went to see him as soon as his studies were completed. "Every new-comer is nervous," Shaikh Farid remarked on seeing that the young man

(33) A reciter of mystic verses.

was unable to speak from fear. Shaikh Nizamuddin shaved his head and was enrolled among the disciples. He was, of course, absolutely penniless; a kindly lady washed his clothes when they became too dirty to be worn any longer, and Shaikh Farid presented him with a gold coin when he was about to leave for Delhi. But it was the last coin of Shaikh Farid's own household, and that very evening Shaikh Nizamuddin discovered that his master and his master's family would have to go without dinner because they lacked the means of purchasing it. The disciple laid the master's gift again at his feet. It was gratefully accepted. "I have prayed to God to grant you a portion of earthly good," Shaikh Farid blessed the young disciple, and then seeing his anxiety added, "Have no fear about it; *for you the world shall not be a temptation.*" The master's discerning eyes had not failed to see the greatness of his successor.

There have been distinguished men in all religions whose life has been a continuous struggle against the world, the flesh and the devil—who have fought and, to a considerable extent, succeeded in the great battle that is supposed to be constantly raging between the higher and the lower elements of human nature. Shaikh Nizamuddin was *not* one of them. He is not recorded to have recited a surprising number of prayers; he did not, like Shaikh Farid, hang himself by his feet in a well or bring himself to the verge of death by unending fasts. There was no element of asceticism in him, because for him the ascetic discipline was not necessary. He did not exorcise the devil by torture or self-mortification, which very often only substitutes morbidity for worldliness, but ruled him out by the quiet joy that inspired his heart. He never married and never possessed a house of his own. People observed that his eyes were red in the morning after his night-long meditation, like one slightly tipsy, and an indescribable happiness shone on his face. There was nothing in the external circumstances of his life to explain this inner bliss.

"I have given you the spiritual empire of Hindustan," Shaikh Farid had ordered him, "Go and take it." But Shaikh Nizamuddin, on returning to Delhi, was for long undecided as to whether he should remain at the capital or select a provincial town for his residence. This is the only inner struggle that seems to have taken place in his mind; but ultimately he decided to face his duty boldly by living and working in the great metropolis. There followed over thirty years of appalling poverty. He first stayed in the house of 'Imadul Mulk, Amir Khusrau's maternal grandfather, who was generally known as the *Rawat-i Arz,* but after two years 'Imadul Mulk's sons returned to Delhi and summarily evicted the Shaikh from their house. He sought refuge in a thatched mosque near by, and that very night 'Imadul Mulk's house caught fire and was burnt to ashes. Thereafter, till his final settlement at Ghiaspur, he kept wandering from one quarter of the city to another. He had no means of his own and never condescended to ask anyone for help. "In the days of Ghiasuddin Balban," the Shaikh used to say in later life, "melons were sold at the rate of one *jital* per maund, but very often the season passed away without my being able to taste a slice............ On one occasion I had to go without food for a night and a day, and half the second night had passed before I got anything to eat; two seers of bread could be had for a *jital,* but from sheer poverty I was unable to purchase anything in the market. My mother, sister and other persons in my house suffered along with me. On one occasion we had starved for three days when a man knocked at my door with a bowl of *khichri.*(34) I have never found anything so delicious as that plain *khichri* appeared to me then. 'We are the guests of God to-day,' my mother used to say when we had no food left in the house, and an inexplicable joy overpowered my heart at these words. Once I dreamt that Shaikh Najibuddin Mutawakkil, brother of Shaikh Farid, had come to our house, and I asked my mother to get something for him to eat. 'But there is no food in our house,' she replied. Soon after I dreamt that the Holy Prophet was coming with his Companions. I kissed his feet and requested him to visit my house. 'What for?' 'I will place before you and your Companions whatever dinner I can provide.' 'But has not your mother told you just now that there is no food in your house?' the Prophet replied. I felt thoroughly ashamed at my position." The venerable mother bore everything bravely along with her son, whose peace of mind no earthly misfortunes could disturb, but the continued starvation was, perhaps, too much for her health. "Whose feet

(34) A simple dish of lentil boiled with rice.

will you kiss next month, Nizam?" she asked him during her last illness when he had placed his head on her feet after seeing the new moon. "And to whose care will you assign me, mother?" the son inquired. Before the morning had dawned she called him to her bed-side. "Almighty God!"—she took his hand in hers—"I assign my son to Thy care." And with these words on her lips the venerable lady passed away.

Meanwhile the Shaikh's fame had been spreading far and wide, and everyone who came in contact with him was captivated by the strange joy that radiated from him. In 1267 A.D. Shaikh Farid nominated him his successor and, just before his death, ordered his cloak, staff and prayer-carpet to be conveyed to Shaikh Nizamuddin, to the intense annoyance of his own children, who expected to succeed to the profitable post. Sultan Jalaluddin offered to endow a village for the Shaikh's expenses; the disciples who had collected round him protested that they had suffered as much as they could stand, but in spite of their protests the offer was firmly refused. The Sultan next asked for an interview; it was not granted; and when the Sultan resolved to pay a surprise visit, the Shaikh, who had come to know of his intention from Amir Khusrau, avoided the interview by undertaking a journey to Ajodhan. The Shaikh had made up his mind to keep aloof from politics, and nothing could turn him from that resolution. But it was impossible for the teacher, who had opened his door wide to all who came, to keep politicians away. In the beginning of Alauddin's reign the nobles began to visit his monastery at Ghiaspur; the Shaikh was annoyed at their visits, but did not refuse to see them. Gradually their number increased. Toward the end of Alauddin's reign the Shaikh's reputation reached its full height. Khizr Khan, the heir-apparent, became a firm believer in the Shaikh, and every member of the Imperial family and every servant of the Palace joined the great discipleship. The Sultan himself was the only exception. "What sort of heart was Alauddin's?" the pious Barni remarks, "How indifferent and bold! From thousands of *farsangs* travellers and students came to pay their respects to the Shaikh; the young and old of the city, scholars and common people, the wise and the foolish, all tried by thousands of tricks to present themselves before him; but it never came to Alauddin's mind that he, too, should either visit the Shaikh or invite him to the Court."(35) The Emperor and the Shaikh were, in fact, too great in their own departments to have anything more than a

---

(35) In the face of Barni's assertion, Amir Khurd's statement, that Alauddin wished to see the Shaikh, but the latter refused to see him and declared that he would leave his house by one door as the Emperor entered it by the other, cannot be accepted. Alauddin, who had an innate suspicion of the political ambitions of religious men—a suspicion not unjustified in many cases—wrote a letter to the Shaikh and offered to be guided by his advice in all matters. But Shaikh Nizamuddin did not even care to open the letter, which was given to him by Khizr Khan. "We, *durweshes*, have nothing to do with the affairs of the state," he replied; "I have settled in a corner apart from the men of the City and spend my time in praying for the Sultan and other Mussalmans. If the Sultan does not like it, let him tell me so. I will go and live elsewhere. God's earth is extensive enough." The reply convinced Alauddin that the Shaikh had no political ambitions.

distant respect for each other. Alauddin cared as little for saints as the Shaikh did for politicians. In his own erratic way he had made up his mind to bend his sinful knees before God alone.

Thanks to the *malfuzats* of Amir Khusrau and Amir Hasan and the *Siyarul Aulia* of Amir Khurd, Shaikh Nizamuddin, at the fulness of his reputation and influence, is better known to us than any other figure in mediæval India. "He opened wide the doors of his discipleship and confessed all sinners—nobles and commons, rich and poor, *maliks* and beggars, students and illiterate folk, citizens and villagers, soldiers and civilians, free-men and slaves." Forenoon and afternoon and the hours after sunset were set apart for those who came to consult him; but he was always accessible and seldom kept anyone waiting. The work of a Shaikh was to educate the people in virtue and goodness, and to this task Shaikh Nizamuddin applied himself with singular devotion throughout his long and useful life. People of every class came to his monastery and he talked to each according to his knowledge and understanding; and everyone who visited the Shaikh felt himself captivated."(36) Besides a thin volume of *malfuzat*, Shaikh Nizamuddin never cared to write anything, and the surviving works of his disciples can but dimly give us the impression of a personality which was as unique as it was fascinating. No Indo-Muslim mystic has left such a deep impression on his contemporaries. "No deed will bring a greater reward on the Day of Judgment," he

---

(36) *Siyarul Aulia.*

used to say, "than bringing hapiness to the hearts of Mussalmans and of men." And yet, in spite of the fact that he was mixing and talking with all who came, people felt that the Shaikh's heart was always "turned towards God as if He was looking at him."(37) The annals of hagiology are strewn with the records of meaningless miracles, but Shaikh Nizamuddin was not a miracle-monger of the ordinary sort. He never flew in the air or walked on water with dry and motionless feet. His greatness was the greatness of a loving heart; his miracles were the miracles of a deeply sympathetic soul. He could read a man's inner heart by a glance at his face and spoke the words that brought consolation to tortured hearts. (1) Khwaja Mubarak of Gopamau used to get a robe of honour from Sultan Alauddin whenever he presented himself at the Court, but on one occasion the Sultan only bestowed a white sheet on him, and the Khwaja, greatly pained at this change in the Sultan's attitude, came to see Shaikh Nizamuddin. The latter looked at him tenderly and said: "A king's gift is a thing of value, be it a gold coin or a shell." "My heart rejoiced at the words," the Khwaja declared later, "and my despondency disappeared." (2) A young sceptic once presented himself with his friends before the Shaikh, and along with the sweet-meats brought by his friends, he placed a little sand wrapped in a paper before the Shaikh. When the servants came to remove the presents, the Shaikh ordered them to leave the packet of sand where it was. "This antimony," he said, "is

---

(37) *Ka-annahu mutawajjihan ilah-i.*

specially meant for my eyes." The young man trembled and confessed, but the Shaikh presented him with a dress and tried to console him. "If you are in need of food or money," he asked, "tell me so and I will do what I can." (3) In the period of his poverty the Shaikh once sat down to eat a few crumbs of bread after he had gone without food for two days. But a beggar, who passed that way, imagined that the Shaikh had finished his dinner and very unceremoniously took away the crumbs from the dinner-cloth. The Shaikh smiled cheerfully. "Our sufferings," he said, "must have been accepted by the Lord that He tries us further." (4) A visitor, who saw the Shaikh and his disciples starving, offered to teach him alchemy. But the Shaikh would have none of it. "Mixing colours," he said, "is the work of Christians, and accumulating gold is the task of Jews. We, Mussalmans, do not wish for the goods of this world or the next. We live for the Lord alone."

Call such things miracles, if you please, provided by a miracle is not meant something morally irrational or meaningless. The Shaikh's life was, in fact, the embodiment of what psychological research shall one day prove to be the deepest principle of our human nature: that salvation, or happiness in its highest form, lies not in a war with the attractions of worldly life or in indifference towards them, but in the healthy development of the 'cosmic emotion,' in a sympathetic identification of the individual with his environment, so that the distinction of the *I* and *not-I* disappears in a mystic absorption of the human soul in the Absolute.

God is not so much a Creator to be acknowledged as an Existence to be felt—felt not as an abstraction but as a reality embodied in the living and inanimate creatures around us. And thus salvation is not something to be obtained in the world beyond; it is to be attained by progressive stages, here and now, or it will be never reached at all.(38) The blessing of Shaikh Farid accompanied his disciple throughout his life. "*For him the world was never a temptation.*" When, in later life, presents began to come to Shaikh Nizamuddin from all sides, he distributed them to the needy with a liberal hand, and every Friday the kitchen and pantry were swept clear before the saint went for his prayer. Sumptuous dishes were placed before his visitors, but the saint, who fasted almost every day, dined only on plain bread with some vegetable. And when a follower remonstrated against his continued abstinence, he replied that "while so many poor and miserable men were starving in the mosques and before the shops in the market, it was impossible for a morsel to pass down his throat." His sleep was as meagre as his diet; he slept a little at midday and rested a little before midnight. But after midnight, when every one had gone to bed, the Shaikh locked up the door of his bedroom and kept meditating, reading, praying and reciting verses till the morning. "In silence I

---

(38) Or, as in Kabir, whose character and thought in some respects closely resemble Shaikh Nizamuddin's: "In life deliverance abides. If your bonds are not broken while living, what hope of deliverance in death? If He is found, He is found here; if not, we go but to dwell in the city of death. Kabir says, 'It is the spirit of the quest which helps; I am the slave of the spirit of the quest.'"

and the lamp keep each other company till the break of day; sometime I extinguish it with the coldness of my sighs, at other times I make it burn brighter with the fire of my soul." He had a delightful time of it. "Every night when the morning is approaching," the Shaikh said once, "a verse comes into my mind which brings me great inspiration and delight. This morning I recollected these lines:—

'The garment by Thy separation torn (39)
Living, once more, once more, re-knit I must.
And if I die, accept my frank excuse,
'Alas, the hopes that crumble into dust!'

But when I was reciting the verses a second time, a woman appeared before me and with great humility requested me not to continue the recitation." "Was it in a dream?" asked one Qazi Sharfuddin. "No, I was wide awake," answered the Shaikh, "I saw her as clearly as I see you." "Then this woman was the symbol of the world which did not wish you to leave her," the Qazi remarked. "You are right," said the Shaikh.

Amir Khusrau became a disciple of the Shaikh when he was only eight years of age, and the Shaikh is said to have encouraged him in his early devotion to poetry. But during the earlier part of his career Khusrau was often absent from Delhi, and the doxology of the *Qiranus Sa'dain,* which was written in the last year of Kai-Kabad's reign, does not refer to

---

(39) *i.e.,* the heart wounded by separation from the Lord. (*Shi'rul Ajam* and *Siyarul Aulia.*)

Shaikh Nizamuddin. The friendship of the Shaikh and the poet probably began in the reign of Sultan Jalaluddin and became closer every day. Though their characters differed widely, there was a strong bond of sympathy between them. Khusrau, in spite of a life spent in the atmosphere of royal courts, was at heart a mystic; and the Shaikh, who often composed quatrains of a very high order, could not but be captivated by the fervour of 'Khusrau's Turkish soul.' The poet, once the heat of youth was over, sat down to a pious life of continued devotions, and the saint, whose tolerance knew no limits, warmly welcomed the courtier who brought into his quiet monastery the refreshing breeze of a different world. "Khusrau, what news?" he would often ask as he leaned on his pillow after dinner and joyfully shook his aged head, while the poet, who had the gossip of Delhi at his fingers' tips, regaled him with the description of a social world, in which the saint took the keen and philanthropic interest of an outsider. Khusrau, on his part, was dazzled by the Shaikh's spiritual grandeur. His whole life had been inspired by a torturing ambition to immortalise himself by a lasting monument of poetry and art. In the Shaikh he came across one who was above such mundane ambitions, and who taught him to feel that the inner development of the spirit was of much greater significance than any external achievement. What men do is less important than what they become; by its own qualities is the human soul to be judged. Khusrau never laid aside his old ideal, but a thousand mellifluous *ghazals* testified to the strength and the 'blessedness' of the new vision. Of course, Khusrau, the panegyrist, could not forget the master to whom he owed so much, and Shaikh Nizamuddin is praised in the doxology of all his later *masnavis.* His name comes even before the name of the Sultan.

But in spite of all his efforts, Shaikh Nizumuddin could not quite keep out of the whirlpool of politics. Sultan Alauddin's eldest son, Khizr Khan, was a disciple of the Shaikh, and it was naturally imagined that the Shaikh would favour his succession. But in the intrigues that followed Alauddin's death, Shaikh Nizamuddin kept quiet. Sultan Kutbuddin Mubarak Shah, who ascended the throne of his father after an interregnum of forty days, at first followed a liberal policy and showed no hostility towards the Shaikh; but, while returning from his Deccan campaign, Mubarak discovered a dastardly conspiracy organised by Malik Asaduddin, a cousin of Sultan Alauddin, and his hand fell heavily on the conspirators. Even the late Sultan's sons, Khizr Khan, Shadi Khan and Shahabuddin, who had been blinded and imprisoned by Malik Kafur at Gwalior, were put to death, and Mubarak felt that he should nurse a grievance against the Shaikh. "He began to speak ill of the Shaikh," Barni tells us, "and displayed open hostility. The *maliks* and *amirs* of the Court were ordered not to go to the Shaikh's monastery at Ghiaspur, and the intoxicated Sultan would often declare with his fearless tongue that he was prepared to give a thousand *tankas* of gold to anyone who brought him Shaikh Nizamuddin's head." Sultan and Shaikh once came face to face at the *siyyum* of Shaikh Ziauddin Rumi, but Mubarak paid no regard to the Shaikh's dignity and even refrained from acknowledging his *salam*. Shaikh Ruknuddin was called from Multan in order to turn away the public eye from Shaikh Nizamuddin Aulia; but as he was an old friend of Shaikh Nizamuddin, Mubarak Shah tried to set up one Shaikhzada Jam, an old enemy of Shaikh Nizamuddin, as a sort of anti-pope. When people are inclined to quarrel, it is easy to find occasions for doing so. The Sultan built a mosque, called the Masjid-i Miri, and invited the leading men of the capital to the first Friday prayer. The Shaikh refused to go. "The mosque nearest my house," he told the Sultan's messenger, "has greater claims on me." Worse than that, the Shaikh ventured to disregard the custom, which required all men of note to attend the Sultan's Court on the first day of every month, and sent his servant, Iqbal, as his deputy. The Sultan naturally resented the insult and finally threatened to call the Shaikh in person by a legal summons as soon as the new moon was seen. But the occasion for it never arrived. On the night of the new moon Mubarak Shah was assassinated by the Barwars, and Shaik Nizamuddin was set free from a difficult situation. The murder of the Sultan, the pious Amir Khurd would have us believe, was due to the prayers of the Shaikh, not to the crimes of the Barwars. The decision of such problems is, fortunately, beyond the province of the historian.

In spite of the friction between the Sultan and his spiritual guide, Khusrau kept on good terms with both. Mubarak treated Khusrau more generously than his father had done, and the poet, in grateful acknowledgment of the favours he had received, composed the *Nuh Sipahr* (Nine Heavens), a versified history of the principal events of Mubarak's reign. The Barwar *regime,* which followed Mubarak's death, was turbulent and short-lived, but Ghiasuddin Tughlak, who mounted the throne after suppressing the rebels, proved to be an ideal ruler according to the needs of the time. He had passed years of apprenticeship in the civil and military service of the state. His personal life was chaste and pure and he was entirely free from that presumptuous arrogance which is often found in self-made men. "Before a week had passed," Ziauddin Barni says, "Ghiasuddin had so effectually removed all traces of disorder, that men imagined that Sultan Alauddin had come to life again." The harsher features of Alauddin's *regime* were removed, but the great reforms were preserved. With such a Sultan Amir Khusrau felt himself in close sympathy, and the *Tughlak Namah,* the last of his historical *masnavis,* bears witness to his admiration for the last of his many patrons. When Ghiasuddin invaded Bengal, the poet accompanied him, and, during his absence, Shaikh Nizamuddin died at Delhi.(40) Khusrau, on his

(40) Shaikh Nizamuddin's relations with Sultan Ghiasuddin also are said to have been none too cordial; so at least later writers would have us believe. Ferishta, who sums up all that he found floating down the stream of time, gives two reasons for this. Khusrau Khan, in his attempt

return, mourned deeply for the friend and guide to whom he had been so very dear. "Pray for my life," the Shaikh had said to him, "for you will not be able to survive me long." The prophecy came true. Khusrau died before six months had elapsed and was buried at his master's feet.

"I want no monument over my grave; lay me to rest in the broad and open plain," Shaikh Nizamuddin had said before his death, but Sultan Mohammad Tughlak, none the less, built a dome over it. Six

---

to find supporters in every direction, distributed large sums of money to distinguished mystics. Three of them refused; others accepted the money but kept it safely in order to give it back to the legitimate king whenever he should appear. But Shaikh Nizamuddin, who had been offered 500,000 *tankas* while other mystics only got 300,000 *tankas* each, immediately took the money and distributed it to the poor. Ghiasuddin recovered most of the money Khusrau Khan had thrown away; all other mystics paid up, but nothing could be recovered from Shaikh Nizamuddin, for the simple reason that nothing was left. This incident is said to have alienated Sultan Ghiasuddin's mind. He also objected to the Shaikh's listening to mystic verses recited by *qawwals,* though, after a learned discussion among scholars, the Sultan withdrew his objection. When returning from the Bengal expedition, Ghiasuddin sent a message to the Shaikh asking him to leave Delhi before the Sultan's return. "Delhi is still far off (*Hanauz Dehli dur ast*)," the Shaikh replied, and the Sultan never reached Delhi. The fall of a mysterious pavilion built for his reception by his son, Mohammad bin Tughlaq, cut short one of the most promising reigns of mediæval India. The incident is quoted by shallow critics as an evidence of the Shaikh's spiritual power. The truth is more tragic. Shaikh Nizamuddin had already departed for 'the world beyond' several days before the Sultan's funeral procession entered Delhi. The story, whatever its moral worth, appears a latter-day fabrication. Neither Barni nor Amir Khurd says anything concerning the unpleasantness between the two old men, who were so eminently virtuous in their different spheres of life.

hundred years have elapsed since; empires have risen and fallen; Delhi has been repeatedly destroyed and rebuilt; but, throughout all these changes, the mausoleum of Shaikh Nizamuddin has remained the one living spot in a city of desolate and crumbling ruins. It is frequented by Hindus and Mussalmans alike.

CHAPTER II

POETICAL WORKS

Amir Khusrau's voluminous works naturally fall into five groups—(1) The Miscellaneous Pieces: *Badi'ul 'Ajaib, Khaliq Bari, Masnavi Shahr Ashub, Chistan* and the Hindi verses; (2) The Historical *Masnavis*: *Qiranus Sa'dain, Miftahul Futuh, Dawal Rani Khizr Khan, Nuh Sipahr* and the *Tughlaq Namah;* (3) The Romantic *Masnavis*: *Matla'ul Anwar, Shirin Khusrau, Aina-i Sikandari, Majnun Laila* and the *Hasht Bihist;* (4) The four *Diwans* or collections of *Ghazals*: *Tuhfatus Sighar, Wastul Laila* and the *Hasht Bihisht;* (4) The four *Diwans* or The Prose Works: *'Ijaz-i Khusravi* and *Khazainul Futuh.*

The miscellaneous pieces need not detain us for long.[1] Khusrau, like several other poets, was fond

---

(1) A number of these miscellaneous pieces have been collected together and printed in a single volume, styled the *La'li 'Umman,* by the Aligarh Muslim University. Students of Khusrau will long be grateful to the late Nawab Mohammad Ishaq Khan Sahib, Secretary of the M. A.-O. College, for his efforts to preserve our author's works. In addition to the *La'li 'Umman,* the *Dawal Rani, Aina-i Sikandari, Majnun Laila* and *Hasht Bihisht* have been excellently lithographed. The *Diwans* (except for a selection by the Newal Kishore Press), the *Miftahul Futuh,* the *Nuh Sipahr* and the *Tughlaq Namah* have not been printed. The *Khazainul Futuh,* edited by Syed Moinul Haq, has been published by the Aligarh Muslim University Historical Society.

of beguiling his idle hours by writing things for children and ordinary people; such compositions show the keenness of his wit and his mastery of words but nothing more. The *Badi'ul 'Ajaib* is a versified, colloquial Arabic-Persian dictionary, while the *Khaliq Bari* is a Hindi-Persian dictionary of the same sort. Both are works of small compass and lay no claim to any poetic merit. In days gone by such compositions had a useful place in our educational system; children learnt them by heart and acquired a small stock of words with which to start their study of a foreign language. The *Masnavi Shahr Ashub,* otherwise known as *Rubaiyat Peshawaran,* is a collection of Persian and Hindi love quatrains addressed to the artisan boys of Delhi, in the homosexual sentiment of which contemporaries found nothing to condemn. The *Chistan* (what is it?) is a collection of riddles in Persian and Hindi verse, meant to be propounded when a company of good fellows sat together. Many of them are very clever, and, without the author's suggestion, it would be difficult to find the correct answer. Translation, however, leaves them insipid, *e.g.,* "What is the animal that has no life? It laughs but has no mouth; weeps but has no eyes; cries but has no tongue?" (Answer—The Cloud.) "A basin full of pearls is placed over the heads of all; the basin turns round and round, yet not a pearl falls out of it." (Answer—The Sky.) The authenticity of most of these pieces is doubtful; there are certainly later additions by unknown hands, but a critical examination may be able to discover Khusrau's original work.

These puerile efforts should not be allowed to detract from Khusrau's real eminence as a poet. To few mortals has nature given such exuberant power of poetic expression. In addition to the *qasida,* contemporaries regarded the *masnavi* and the *ghazal* as the best media for the poet's thoughts, and in all these his work is monumental. Prose, as we shall see later, he wrote with difficulty and effort; poetry came to him spontaneously and his speed in writing verse was astonishing. The style of his *masnavis* is simple and graceful; line follows line in an unbroken harmony of sense and music and leaves on the reader a unique impression of the fertility of the author's mind and his command of the language; and the impression is all the more profound because the theme of Khusrau's *masnavis* is often commonplace and prosaic in the extreme. The flow of words carries the critic so smoothly down the stream that he fails to note how often Khusrau is expanding to inordinate length ideas utterly nonsensical and, for most people, too commonplace to be expressed in prose. Stiff and hard as are the rules of Persian versification, the poet moulds his material like wax. It is difficult for any translation to do justice to the original, but the following description, from the *Qiranus Sa'dain,* of a thousand Mongol captives, who were brought and thrown under the feet of the elephants before the throne of Muizzuddin Kai-Kabad, might give the reader some idea of the strength and weakness of Khusrau's *masnavi*:—

"Then the captives taken by the army—a thousand Tatar infidels seated on camels tailwards—were brought for review before the Imperial throne. Headstrong and fierce in battle, they wore cotton garments over their bodies of steel. They had hats of wool over their faces of fire, and it looked as if the fire would set the wool aflame. Their heads were shaved in anticipation of the disgrace that awaited them. Their eyes were like two crevices in a basin of silver, and their eye-balls like flints lying in the cracks of rocks. They stank worse than rotting carcasses, while their heads were bowed as low as their backs. Their skin was crumpled and wrinkled like the moist leather of a kettle-drum. Their nostrils stretched wide from cheek to cheek, and their mouths from one side of their hat to the other. Yes, their nostrils looked like desolated graves or like ovens full of stinking water. The hair of their nostrils spread wide over their lips and their moustaches grew to an inordinate length; nevertheless, their sunken cheeks were unadorned by beards, for no sort of vegetation will grow on a surface of ice............ From excess of lice in their clothes, their breasts had become black and white like mustard grown on a barren soil; but while other people get oil from mustard, in this case the mustard had drawn oil from the bodies of the Tatars. Their backs also had become covered with rough, untanned hide from the continuous stinging of lice, and the skin of their skulls was strong enough to be used for the soles of shoes............ They devoured pigs and dogs with their ugly teeth, though the 'teeth of wisdom' were, indeed, absent from their jaws. They danced to the sound of the pipe like women wailing one after another; they drank the water of sewers and ate tasteless grasses. I have also heard another story about them: if one of them vomits, another will eat the vomit, but this I do not consider strange for they belong to the Turkish tribe of *Qai* (vomit). In any case their food is more horrid than a man's vomit, and anyone who sees it will feel quite sick. Their origin is from dogs but their bones are bigger—and the gravy of cats is served at their dinners. The Emperor wondered at their ugly features as he surveyed the row of large-bodied men seated on the humps of camels. "God must have created them out of hell-fire," he remarked. "There is no might or power in any save Allah!" the people exclaimed as one white demon emerged after another.

"When the captives had been reviewed, a reckoning was taken of the Tatars slain. Their heads stuffed with straw were lifted on the points of spears; even after death they held their heads high, and the spears before the spectator's eye were as innumerable as weeds in a forest of weeds.

"The Emperor then ordered the elephants to be brought so that the wretches might be despatched to their doom. The earth shook and the mountains trembled as the line of elephants advanced and stood before the Emperor like Alexander's wall; the sound of drums and instruments of warlike music rent the air, and the elephants thundered in return like echoes resounding from distant mountains. By the Emperor's orders the cows and the male buffaloes (*i.e.*, Mongol women and men) were tied into pairs and thrown before the elephants. The earth quaked as they fell. Each animal moved forward and lifted them between its tusks with a venomous strength that would have sufficed to lift up the Cow that holds the earth on its horns; next it sent the cow (*i.e.*, the woman) flying into the air with the agility of a mountain goat, while a gurgling sound came out of the Mongol throat as the male and the female were separated from each other. Yes, though the ropes were loosely tied round their necks, nevertheless the cords of life and relationship were snapped asunder; and whatever remained united still, the elephant proceeded to tear apart with its tusks.(2) In spite of their large bones they were squeezed into small size under the elephant's feet. The Emperor next commanded the Mongols to

---

(2) That is, *first*, the Mongols were tied together by the neck in pairs and placed before the elephants. *Next*, the animal, after putting the pair on its tusks, wound its trunk round the woman, tore her apart from the man—hence the gurgling sound from the Mongol throat—and threw her up in the air. The rope round their necks would naturally cut through their necks; but if this did not happen, the elephant, carefully trained to its work, proceeded to sever the head from the body with its tusks. *Lastly*, the headless trunks of the Mongols were tied by the attendants into bundles of ten; and the elephants, after raising these bundles and placing them before the throne, pounded them into meat for beasts and birds by trampling them under their feet. The heads of the Mongols, which still lay on the ground, were thrown about in the air by the elephants.

There were generally a number of elephants at the Emperor's court, who had been carefully trained to do the executioner's work. They were first given pillows to tear and throw about, and it was only after they had successfully passed through the preliminary apprenticeship, that the bodies of human beings were entrusted to them. Throwing under an elephant's feet was an orthodox form of execution in the Middle Ages; but the process did not consist of mere trampling; the animal was required to play about with the doomed person for a good long time before killing him; and it was punished, if through its tactless handling, death came earlier

be tied into bundles of ten; and those who had advanced to battle with tight waist bands, shoulder to shoulder, were now tied stiffly together, back to back and breast to breast. The elephant first took these bundles of Mongols and placed them before the Emperor; then it crushed their bodies beneath its feet while it sent their heads flying in the air like pillows. The captives would have counted themselves fortunate if their heads had been simply cut off. But, no, their heads were raised high and a fine treatment was meted out to their skulls and to their bodies! When some of the 'commanders of hundred' (*amir-i sadah*) had been thus pounded into meat for birds and beasts, the Emperor ordered the rest to be paraded in the city.

"All day the Emperor sat supervising the punishment of the Mongols; in the evening he called for wine."

---

than the programme permitted. The object, apparently, was to subject the unhappy man to the longest possible period of excruciating pain.

Mediæval methods of torture in Europe as well as Asia are a fascinating if somewhat gruesome subject for the historian. Islam prohibits all methods of execution except hanging, beheading and impaling, but so far as traitors and political enemies were concerned, the law was more honoured in the breach than the observance. The Mongols, who were comparatively indifferent to other fine arts, excelled in this; and it was from them that the Indians and other peoples learnt new and curious modes of putting human beings to death. Most historians of the Mongols have described Mongol methods of execution in detail, and the reader, who wants further information, is recommended to consult Howorth's *History of the Mongols,* the *Tarikh-i Jahan Gusha* of Alauddin Ata Malik Juwaini, *Tarikh-i Wassaf* and the last chapter of Minhajus Siraj Jurjani's *Tabaqat-i Nasiri.*

An admirer of Khusrau cannot but regret that in none of his historical *masnavis* did he find a theme suited to his pen. The *Qiranus Sa'dain* (Conjunction of the Two Lucky Planets), his first volume, was composed at the order of Muizzuddin Kai-Kabad and has all the colourless insipidity of a government publication. The metre is soft and sweet and Khusrau's power never flags, while some of the *ghazals* are remarkable for their poetic beauty. Nevertheless, the dull records of one of the most stupid reigns of mediæval India was hardly the proper theme for Khusrau's muse. An artist in a position to express his views would have, no doubt, found much to depict—the tragedy of a handsome young Emperor of eighteen drinking himself to death in spite of the futile advice of a futile father taken out of a silly, old text-book on politics; the ambition and incompetence of the *wazir;* the intrigues of the Turkish nobility, who combined some of the best and some of the worst traits of human nature; and below their feet the rumblings of an approaching revolution, which was soon to cast everything into the furnace and mould it anew. Human life is always full of humour and tragedy, if we will but see it in the proper perspective. Khusrau, however, was prevented from making a poetic use of his material by the very purpose of his work; things had to be surveyed from the official, not the artistic, view-point; and this made the production of a real poem impossible. There is here, as elsewhere, no lack of verbal ingenuity and verbal trickery and quaint turns of thought and figures of speech, that delighted his contemporaries but are wearisome to our modern taste. Of these superficial beauties Khusrau has always enough and to spare; but the desire of earning the material rewards for an official poem beguiled the poet, who could appreciate every human emotion from the grossest passion to the highest spiritual ecstasy, into wasting his energies on a topic which no genius could prevent from being dull and wearisome. He praises Delhi and its artists; its tank, fort and mosque; finds something to say about the Emperor's canopy, baton, sword and arrow; details the correspondence between Kai-Kabad and his father at great length; and thus by tagging miscellaneous scraps together manages to produce a volume of two hundred and fifty pages, in which the student of history will find precious little information about the annals of the reign and the student of poetry little that has any genuine, human value.

The defects of the *Qiranus Sa'dain* reappear, in a greater or lesser degree, in Khusrau's other historical *masnavis*. But the *Miftahul Futuh,*(3) the second volume of the series, is distinguished by its solid historical worth. Khusrau had a genuine affection for the veteran soldier, Sultan Jalaluddin, whose reign he chronicled, and gives us here a clear and detailed account of his four campaigns. The poet himself was an officer acquainted with military tactics; Jalaluddin's sobriety and good sense made flattery unnecessary; and Khusrau thought that he would please his master best by adhering to truth. There is thus presented

(3) Key of Conquests.

to us a volume which might have with advantage been in simple prose. But Khusrau's verse does not lack simplicity and directness of expression, and in spite of its rhyme and metre, the *Miftahul Futuh* will be found invaluable by a student of the military history of India.

The *Dawal Rani Khizr Khan,* the third and best of Amir Khusrau's historical *masnavis,* deserves a more detailed notice. In their attempt to imitate or rival their predecessors, Indo-Persian poets have endowed their productions with an artificiality and verbosity, which can only be admired by readers who have never tasted better fare. From this misfortune the *Dawal Rani* was saved by a train of unhappy events which provided our poet with material for a romance as tragic as it is human. Sultan Alauddin's eldest son, Khizr Khan, in the trying days when he had been separated from Dawal Rani and could seldom manage to see her, called Khusrau to his Court and confided the secret of his heart to the poet. "I am consumed with a youthful passion, of which you know already. All day I pine like Majnun and my sleepless nights are passed in dreaming of my Laila. I have lost my way in a wilderness where Khizr himself, the guide of travellers, could not find his path. I wish you to weave my secret romance into a poem that may bring the dead to life." A servant placed a draft of the story, written by the Khan himself, in the poet's hand. Khusrau readily undertook the task and promised to do his best.

The doxology of the *Dawal Rani* contains the usual praises of God, "the creator of all lovely things, who has attached the human heart to beauty and created the maidens of China and Khorasan for the excitement of love." Next come praises of the Apostle, "who, while Heaven had opened its nine doors wide for him, prided himself on a poor man's cottage"; of the Four Caliphs and of Shaikh Nizam-uddin, "whose heart is the treasury of divine love." Sultan Alauddin, though he is mentioned after the poet's spiritual chief, nevertheless occupies a prominent place. "The Mongols are so afraid of him that even their pictures refuse to venture into this country, when the artist tries to paint them. His arrow, like a clever and beautiful maiden, has deprived the Hindu *rais* of their hearts (courage)........... He crushes the headstrong but cherishes the weak...........and the people are happy in his reign like school-boys on a holiday." In the enthusiasm of his loyalty the poet even presumes to advise the Emperor on affairs of state. But the subject is tactfully broached. "The Emperor knew his work better than others could tell him. Still, it was the duty of his faithful servants to offer him the best counsel they could." "If you desire the permanence of your empire, base it on the good-will of the people. Put rebels to death, for this is permissible, but be kind in your dealings with others; keep your mind awake and your sword asleep. When your own feet are injured by walking on rose-petals, do not place thorns in the path of others. Be not vain; you are but a particle of dust in the storm and imagine yourself a mountain. These pleasant dreams are well, provided they do not conflict with reality. Your political achievements are not trifling; they are, in fact, stupendous; but their inspiring motive has been your own personal gain. People complain to the Emperor of the injustice of others; but if the Emperor is himself unjust, to whom are they to carry their complaint? Royal power is based on justice and fair dealing. The financial stability of the state depends on the prosperity of the *ra'iyat;* when the *ra'iyat* is ruined, the state will be ruined also. And if the army does not receive its pay regularly.........who will carry the load when the camel is dead? Kings are not made of different clay from the common people, nor is happiness an exclusive privilege of royalty. We are gems from the same mine; why, then, should there be any distinction between us? If the Emperor's bridle is as high as the heaven, the prayers of the injured rise higher still. A ruler should see with both his eyes—the eye of mercy and the eye of justice—and then all his affairs will be managed well. But if the shepherd of the people drinks to excess, his intoxication is sure to injure the flock. Music, songs and other amusements should be indulged in with moderation, for too much devotion to the songs of David is sure to ruin Solomon's throne." There follows next a brief account of the Sultans of Delhi and a sketchy, but valuable, review of Alauddin's campaigns.

It is by tagging together miscellaneous pieces such as these that Khusrau used to produce his historical *masnavis,* and the *Dawal Rani,* as originally planned, was no better. Nevertheless, unlike the *Qiranus Sa'dain* and the *Nuh Sipahr,* which could never rise above the level of mere court annals, it had a human theme and the march of events endowed it with a tragic grandeur. Judging from internal evidence, the *Dawal Rani* was produced in two, possibly more, instalments. Whatever the date of the poet's interview with Khizr Khan, he tells us that he finished the first instalment in 1315 A.D., after four months' labour. Later on, he continued the narrative to Khizr Khan's death and there are a few lines which could not have been written while Mubarak Shah was alive.

The outline of the romance is of sufficient historic interest to find a place here. The earlier portion has been summarised by Ferishta in prose: "Towards the beginning of the year 697 A.H. (1298 A.D.), the Emperor sent Ulugh Khan and Nusrat Khan with many *amirs* of the Court and the army to conquer Gujerat. They plundered Nahrwala (Anhilwara) and brought the whole of Gujerat under their power. Rai Karan, the ruler of Nahrwala, fled and took refuge with Ram Deo, the Raja of Deogir, in the Deccan; but after a few days he came forward and established himself with Ram Deo's support in the territory of Baglana, which is a part of Gujerat situated on the frontier of the Deccan. The Imperial *amirs* captured Rai Karan's wives, the chief of whom was Kaunladi,(4) along with his treasures and elephants. After Sultan Mahmud Ghaznavi's destruction of Somnath, the Brahmans had constructed another idol in its place, which they worshipped and renamed Somnath; this was sent to Delhi to be trampled under

(4) Her real name seems to have been Kamala Devi, a name quite common in Gujerat, and of her daughter, Diwal Devi, but they have been Persianised into Kaunladi and Diwaldi or Dawal Rani.

the feet of the people. Then Nusrat Khan advanced to Kambhayat and exacted money and jewels beyond reckoning from the inhabitants of that place. He also forcibly took Kafur Hazardinari from his *Khwaja* (master). This Kafur was ultimately appointed Regent of the Empire by the Emperor and given the title of *Malik Naib*............

" Ram Deo, the ruler of Deogir, having rebelled and refrained from sending any presents for three years, Alauddin appointed the *Malik Naib* Kafur Hazardinari with many famous *amirs* for the conquest of southern territories, known in the terminology of Hind as the 'Deccan.' The Emperor was infatuated with the *Malik Naib* and wished to exalt him to an unquestioned superiority over all other officers, so that they might render him due obedience. Consequently, he bestowed on his favourite the canopy and red tent, which was the peculiar prerogative of the Emperors of Delhi. All *amirs* and officers were directed to present themselves before him every day and to execute his orders without any deviation. Khwaja Haji, the *Naib-i Arz-i Mumalik,* a gentle and virtuous man, was sent with him to look after the army and collect the spoils. According to Qazi Ahmed Ghaffari, the author of *Nushka-i Jehan Ara,* the *Malik Naib* and Khwaja Haji started for the Deccan towards the beginning of 706 A.H. (1306 A.D.) with a hundred thousand horse. A *firman* was sent to Malik Ainul Mulk Multani, governor of Malwa, and Ulugh (Alp) Khan, governor of Gujerat, that they were to consider themselves subordinate to the *Malik Naib* and carry out his orders.

"At this moment Kaunladi—before whom the connoisseur lost his colour in shame—represented to the Emperor: 'When I was in the bed-chamber of Rai Karan, I had two fairy-faced daughters in my arms, whom I cherished as the morning breeze cherishes the rose. When my good fortune placed me among the worshippers of the Emperor, both my pearls (daughters) were left with the Rai. Now, I hear, that by the order of God the elder daughter has descended into the bosom of the earth. The other, named Diwaldi (Diwal Devi), whom I have not seen for four years, is still reposing on the bed of life. If the *Malik Naib* and Khwaja Haji are ordered to send that particle (Diwal Devi) to the Sun of the State (the Court) it will be a great kindness and favour.' The Emperor, on hearing the request, sent a *firman* to the *Malik Naib* and Alp Khan: 'They were to take from Rai Karan, who was residing in the Deccan, his daughter, Diwaldi, whether he gave her up willingly or through force, and send her to the Court.'

"The *Malik Naib* crossed Malwa and appeared on the frontier of the Deccan. From here, through wise messengers, he sent the Emperor's *firmans* to Ram Deo, Rai Karan and all the *rais* of the South. The drift of the *firmans* suggests that he was then staying at the towns of Sultanpur and Nadbar. Be this as it may, the *rais* having failed to promise any sort of obedience, the *Malik Naib* started from Sultanpur and crossed the frontier of the Deccan. Alp Khan also moved forward with a large army from Gujerat towards the hills of Baglana. But Rai Karan had strengthened his positions and held them firmly for two months. There were many engagements between him and Ulugh Khan but he emerged stronger from every encounter. Now Sangal Deo, son of Ram Deo, had for long desired to marry Dilwaldi, but Rai Karan, being a Rajput, was unwilling to marry his daughter to a Mahratta. At this juncture Sangal Deo found his opportunity. Without his father's permission, he sent his younger brother, Bhim Deo, with presents to Rai Karan. 'There is a great difference of religion,' was his message, 'between the infidels and the Turks. If you consent to my marriage with your daughter, who is the object of all this struggle, the Mussalmans will refrain from molesting you and will go back.' Rai Karan, who was in need of Mahratta help, perforce agreed to the proposal. He married the fairy to the demon (*deo*) and wished to send her to Deogir with Bhim Deo.

"Alp Khan was greatly disturbed by this turn of events and trembled like a reed from fear of Alauddin's anger. He called a council and discussed the matter with his *amirs*. 'The best course for us, while Diwaldi is still here,' he suggested, 'is to get the desired pearl into our hands at daybreak, or else die in this desert without showing our faces to the Emperor again.' To this the *amirs* agreed. They came to the hills with a united heart and fought desperately. Rai Karan suffered a severe defeat, and leaving all his elephants and horses, fled to Deogir like the wind. Alp Khan followed him like lightning over hill and plain, but at a day's march from Deogir, the hope of his heart disappeared from his eyesight. Nevertheless Alauddin's good fortune worked its way, Dilwaldi was captured in a strange manner, and those who believed that Alauddin possessed miraculous powers became louder in their assertions. Briefly, the incident occurred thus. When Alp Khan gave up all hopes of overtaking Rai Karan or Dilwaldi, he encamped on the bank of a river and remained there for two days. Some three or four hundred young men, who had heard of the Ellora Hill, which is situated near Deogir, went to visit it with Alp Khan's permission. While wandering about the place, they suddenly saw an army of the southern people, and imagining that Ram Deo had fallen upon them, they collected together and stood in ranks before the enemy. But it was really Bhim Deo, who had separated from Rai Karan's army and was taking Diwaldi to his brother. The two parties joined battle, but the Hindus, unable to bear the anvil-piercing arrows of the Mongols, Khiljis, etc., took to flight. An arrow struck Diwaldi's horse and it was disabled. The young men crowded round her, each trying to possess her for himself. At this moment one of her attendants cried out: 'She is Diwaldi. Be careful of her honour and take her to your chief.' On hearing her name, they took her to Alp Khan with the rapidity of a cloud. Alp Khan was beside himself with joy. He thanked God for his success and started for Gujerat without delay. From there he sent Diwaldi in a litter (*palki*) to Delhi. Towards the end of 706 A.H. (1307 A.D.), she reached the Court to brighten her mother's eyes."

At the Imperial Court the young daughter of Rai Karan was brought up with Khizr Khan, the Sultan's eldest son, and gradually the consciousness of sex-feeling dawned on the two children, who had been allowed to play about together quite freely; it was a remarkable case of calf-love, but contrary to what happens in most such cases, the attachment on both sides grew with years. Khizr Khan's mother had set her heart on marrying him to her brother Alp Khan's daughter. She transferred the pair to separate residences as soon as her suspicions were aroused; but they continued to meet by stealth, and the *Malka-i Jehan*,(5) like most Indian mothers, thought she could solve the problem by hastening Khizr Khan's marriage, which was celebrated with great pomp. The ceremony was a painful ordeal for the young prince, who was compelled to accept his cousin for his bride while his heart longed for Dawal Rani; and, as might have been foreseen, it only made matters worse. Khizr Khan could not, or would not, take to his wife and kept pining for the girl to whom he had secretly plighted his troth. The elderly ladies of the palace drew the *Malka-i Jehan's* attention to the gravity of the situation. "Would she sacrifice her son for the sake of her niece?" A mother's instinct could not long hesitate in making a choice, and she allowed Khizr Khan and Dawal Rani to be quietly married.

Unfortunately, Khizr Khan proved to be a lover and no more, and contemporaries saw nothing in him

---

(5) The Emperor's principal wife was called the *Malka-i Jehan* (Queen of the World) and the Emperor was addressed as *Khudawand-i 'Alam* (Master of the World).

except a thoughtless devotion to pleasure. He was utterly ignorant of the business of the state, and, after his marriage with Dawal Rani, he fell into the hands of profligate companions. It was not for such an heir that Alauddin had longed, and in spite of his paternal affection, his mind turned away decisively from the son, who was unable to walk in his footsteps.

"Meanwhile the Sultan," Ferishta continues, "had fallen into a dangerous illness.(6) But as Khizr Khan and the *Malka-i Jehan* were all the time busy with their unending revelries and feasts, they failed to look after him. The Emperor thought he did not regain his health owing to their neglect and his heart was deeply offended. Every day they did something to increase his anger and suspicion. Khizr Khan had no other business besides holding entertainments, drinking wine, hearing songs and music, playing *chaugan* (polo) and watching elephant fights; his mother, too, devoted all her time to the festivals she arranged in honour of the marriages, *sar-tarashi* (7) and circumcision of her sons: the one thing they never cared for was Sultan Alauddin and his illness. So the Sultan called the *Malik Naib* from Deogir and Alp Khan from Gujerat, and was greatly pleased at their quick arrival. He complained of his wife and son to the *Malik Naib* in private; and the latter, who had already formed ambitions for the kingdom, found this a welcome opportunity. 'Both of them are plotting with Alp Khan to put you to death,' he said, 'they are waiting

---

(6) Barni says it was dropsy (*istisqa*).

(7) Ceremony of first shaving an infant's head.

for your Majesty's demise.' At this juncture the *Malka-i Jehan* applied for the Emperor's permission to marry Shadi Khan to Alp Khan's daughter. The *Malik Naib* found another opportunity of repeating his dismal warning and Alauddin grew suspicious. As a measure of caution he sent Khizr Khan to Amroha on an expedition of hunting and pleasure. 'I will recall you as soon as I have regained my health,' the Emperor promised his son; and Khizr Khan, on his part, made a vow that if his father recovered, he would come barefooted to visit the saints of Delhi. Consequently, as soon as he heard of his father's recovery, Khizr Khan started barefooted with his troops for Delhi before an order of recall could reach him. The *Malik Naib* again found his opportunity. 'As Khizr Khan has come without permission,' he represented to the Sultan, 'it is necessary to be on guard against him, lest in alliance with the *amirs*, he may begin to harbour evil intentions.' The Emperor did not believe this at first. He called Khizr Khan to his presence, showed him every mark of paternal affection, took him in his arms, kissed his forehead and eyes, and then allowed him to go to the *harem* to see his mother and sisters. But after a few days Khizr Khan again became careless. He neglected his duties at the Court and went away to his own house. His dangerous rival was now in a position to push on his scheme and succeeded in putting strange suspicions into the Emperor's mind. 'Khizr Khan,' the *Malik Naib* said, 'wishes to make an attempt on your Majesty's life with the help of Shadi Khan and other persons.' He brought forward a body of slaves and palace-eunuchs to confirm his assertion, and by deception and flattery obtained the Emperor's permission to imprison the two brothers, Khizr Khan and Shadi Khan, who were forthwith sent to the fort of Gwalior. At the same time he turned Khizr Khan's mother out of the palace and imprisoned her in Old Delhi."

Alauddin died soon after and the *Malik Naib* placed Shahabuddin 'Umar, the Sultan's youngest son, on the throne. At the same time he sent one, Sumbul, to blind Khizr Khan at Gwalior. The *ex*-heir-apparent's character showed best in misfortunes, and he accepted his fate with a pious resignation. "He sat smiling calmly at the decree of fate instead of attempting to run away from it like a fool. 'Maybe, the Emperor is dead,' he remarked when Sumbul and his men, covered with the dust of the road, appeared before him, 'that disturbances, which had been quelled, are rising again. But why this hurry with which you have come to do me honour in my prison?' His eyes, which were soon to be blinded, were moist with tears. 'I have no hope of regaining my freedom, for who will place his enemy on the throne? But if you have an order for depriving me of my life or my eyesight, I am ready.' Sumbul pleaded that he was a mere instrument in the hands of others and was not personally to blame. 'But the Minister, who was all in all during the late Sultan's reign, wishes to deprive you of your sight.' The prince willingly offered his eyes to Sumbul. They laid him on the ground; and when his eyes were pierced by the needle, the sockets were filled with blood like a wine-glass."(8) Sumbul returned to Delhi in haste to win the rewards promised for his deed, but his master's tenure of power was short. Within forty days of Sultan Alauddin's death, the *Malik Naib* was assassinated by the guards of the Palace, who elevated Mubarak Shah, a son of the late Sultan, to the Regency and, later on, to the throne. A well-wisher carried the news of the *Malik Naib's* death to Khizr Khan in prison. "But the generous-hearted son of the Sultan refused to rejoice at it, for he knew that misfortunes overtake everyone in his turn. He bowed to God in gratitude for His justice, and wept at his own fate and at the fate of the rascal to whom all his misfortunes were due."

For about two years the blinded Khizr Khan lived in the prison-fort of Gwalior, his loneliness (if we are to believe the poet) being considerably lightened by the tender companionship of his beloved Dawal Rani. Then matters suddenly took a tragic turn. While returning from Deogir, Mubarak Shah discovered a conspiracy organised by Yaghrish Khan, a cousin of Sultan Alauddin, and in the wrath of his heart resolved to put all his rivals to death. Anxious to find an execuse, he sent a message to Khizr Khan, promising him freedom and a governorship when the aspect of affairs was quieter and asking him to send Dawal Rani, who had been the cause of all his misfortunes, 'for a time' to the Court. Khizr Khan bluntly refused to obey his brother's order. "My head should be struck off first," he replied. Mubarak flew into a rage and ordered his

(8) I have condensed the passage from the *Dawal Rani*.

head-guardsman, Shadi (joy), 'at whose sight not only joy but sorrow took to flight,' to go and put the princes at Gwalior to death. "A tumult, as of the Day of Resurrection, arose from the veiled inmates of the *harem* when Shadi (9) and his rascals broke into the house of the princes. The princes jumped out of their cells like lions, but their arms were weak and their bodies were powerless. Prince Shadi Khan in his wrath appealed for Divine assistance and flew at the *Kotwal* of the fort. He knocked the *Kotwal* down and then looked round for his sword. But he had long before this been deprived of his conquering sword and all his efforts were futile. The assassins ran to the *Kotwal's* help from every side; they knocked down Shadi Khan and lifted the *Kotwal* from the ground. The two princes were then bound hand and foot. Shadi ordered the prostrate princes to be beheaded, but none of his men would step forward to do the deed. For some moments a strange silence prevailed; ultimately a low-born Hindu came forward from the ranks, tucked up his sleeves, and asking Shadi for his dagger, advanced towards Khizr Khan. The sun and the moon seemed to testify to the oath of affirmation that burst from the victim's lips; the inmates of the prison shrieked in desperation when the dagger flashed; but the unhesitating rascal beheaded the Khan at a single stroke and placed his head by the side of his body."

The human element, which has raised the *Dawal Rani* to a level far above the other *masnavis* of

---

(9) Shadi, the head of Mubarak Shah's guards, must not be confused with Prince Shadi Khan, whom he was commissioned to assassinate.

Khusrau, is conspicuous by its absence in the *Nuh Sipahr* (Nine Heavens), which is a versified history of the reign of Sultan Kutubuddin Mubarak Shah. It had by now become a tradition for every Emperor to request the willing poet for a history of his reign in his inexhaustible and mellifluous verse, and Mubarak Shah is said to have rewarded Khusrau liberally for his labour. The Sultan was not the perverted criminal which he is sometimes said to have been; in spite of the orgies at the Court, the Empire was well governed; the provinces were pacified; rebellion was crushed wherever it appeared; and unlike his elder brother, Khizr Khan, Mubarak Shah had an innate liking for efficiency and work. Nevertheless, Khusrau could not find much to appreciate in the arrogant young monarch; and apart from an account of the Sultan's Deogir campaign, the *Nuh Sipahr* is a formless assortment of miscellaneous odds and ends—a painfully elaborate doxology, praises of Hindustan, a lengthy conversation between the Sultan's bow and arrow, and the like.

Towards the end of his life Khusrau composed the last of his historical *masnavis,* the *Tughlaq Namah,* an account of the reign of Sultan Ghiasuddin Tughlaq. The circle that had collected round Sultan Ghiasuddin's son, Malik Fakhruddin Jauna (later, Sultan Mohammad bin Tughlaq), included some of Khusrau's severest critics. Nevertheless, there was much that Khusrau could applaud in the honest, straightforward character of the founder of the Tughlaq dynasty, who by sheer merit had risen from an humble origin to the highest position in the state and 'wore an elective crown.' In a verse attributed to him by Barni, Khusrau declares that 'Sultan Ghiasuddin did nothing that did not testify to the perfection of his wisdom and knowledge; it seemed as if he had the intellect of a thousand scholars in his single brain.' Unfortunately, the *Tughlaq Namah* has not reached us in a complete form, probably because the author did not live to finish and revise it. He was approaching his seventieth year and survived the Sultan by a few months only. The Emperor Jahangir is said to have ordered a 'reconstruction' of the *Tughlaq Namah;* but its manuscripts are, and have always been, rare.(10)

The romantic *masnavi* of the Persians is a natural development from the *Shah Namah* epic. Even a casual reader cannot fail to be impressed by the enormous length of Firdausi's great work and its lack of artistic construction; the dullest stories are placed side by side with the most sensational and impressive, with no attempt at a critical selection; the poet, like his Ghaznavide contemporaries, can only feel and express the more violent emotions while the lighter shades of feeling are ignored; it is rough-hewn and unchiselled. Surely, the narrative verse was capable of something better, at least of something different and equally good. The poet who first grasped the possibility of

---

(10) The only manuscript I am acquainted with is in possession of Maulvi Obaidur Rahman Khan Sahib, M.L.C., *Rais,* Bhikampur, Aligarh. It is very defective and difficult to decipher. Moulvi Rashid Ahmad Sahib, the editor of *Dawal Rani,* spent a considerable time in editing the *Tughlaq Namah* on the basis of the Bhikampur manuscript and his volume was ready for the press when he died. I do not know what has happened to it. Ferishta tells us that manuscripts of the *Tughlaq Namah* were rare in his day.

a new development in the narrative verse was Shaikh Nizami of Ganja (1139-1200 A.D.). He brought to his task a fertility of mind, which was hardly inferior to Firdausi's, a discriminating sensitiveness of feeling, which Firdausi had lacked, and a critical faculty of selection, which was altogether his own. His poetic outlook was more comprehensive; his power over words was certainly greater, and later critics have loved to call him the 'lord of language' (*khuda-i sukhan*). The *Khamsah* of Nizami stands by the side of the *Shah Namah* like a trim and artistically laid-out modern park by the side of a primeval forest—it has less of tradition but more of art.

The sweetest flowers spring from the soil that has been manured continuously for years, and Nizami, like all great critics, realised that if he wanted a good plot, he could only find it in the ancient folklore of his country. Persia was a soil rich in traditions to which warriors, poets and peasants had all contributed their mites; innumerable anecdotes, stories and fables had clustered round the glorious names of Jamshed and Rustam, Alexander and Bahram, Khusrau and Anusherwan. It was unnecessary for Nizami to create a plot; nothing that he could create would equal in poetic beauty what tradition had already placed within his reach. His duty was to pick and choose, and he chose the very best. Of the five works of Nizami, which are collectively known as the *Khamsah*, the first, *Makhzanul Asrar*, is not a romantic *masnavi* at all. It is a treatise on twenty moral topics, the author's instructions being illustrated by short anecdotes or *hikayats*. The remaining four works—*Shirin Khusrau*,

Majnun Laila, Sikandar Namah and *Haft Paikar*—are romantic *masnavis,* properly so called. The *Sikandar* (Alexander) of Nizami is not the Alexander of history, but of tradition and art; the criminal conqueror from the west is elevated to the status of a Roman Cæsar, of a philosopher and a national Persian hero. The *Laila Majnun* is an Arab legend; it has no war or historic episodes in its tale of forlorn love, and Nizami felt some diffidence in handling it. The *Shirin Khusrau* and *Haft Paikar* embalm the Persian tales that clustered round the Emperors Khusrau and Bahram Gor.

Nizami was one of the acknowledged masters of Persian poetry when Khusrau began to write; he had become as popular as the traditions on which he has impressed his personality for ever. Maulana Shibli tells us that Khusrau began his apprenticeship in poetry by placing the best passages from the masters before himself and trying to model his work on them. If so, Nizami could hardly fail to be one of the classics selected, and Khusrau's work throughout shows how profoundly Nizami had influenced him. But it was not till the beginning of Alauddin's reign that Khusrau conceived the plan of rivalling, and, if possible, of surpassing the great master. His *ghazals* had already made him famous and had even won from the Persians themselves a homage which they seldom yield to any but their countrymen. He had written two historical *masnavis,* the *Qiranus Sa'dain* and *Miftahul Futuh,* which no one in India could pretend to rival. He had patrons, flatterers, friends, and an appreciative public, which had seen no greater genius than his east of the

Indus; and, misled by these external marks of success, he began his task in a spirit of superb self-confidence. "When my ambition first moved its charger towards the sky," he says in the beginning of his first romantic *masnavi*, the *Matla'ul Anwar*, "fortune granted me all her treasures. Every work I attempted turned out to be better than I had hoped............ The fame of my eminence rose and reverberated in Nizami's grave. Maybe, the seal of perfection has been impressed on Nizami's work, but the coins I am manufacturing will break that seal; the poet of Ganja has won immortal fame through his five treasures (*masnavis*), but I will make five keys to open his five treasures and compete with him for the domain, over which he has held sway so long............ Yes, such shall be the excellence of my *masnavis* that even the most discerning critic will not be able to distinguish his work from mine."

Khusrau's romantic *masnavis*, collectively known as the *Panj Ganj*, are closely modelled on Nizami's *Khamsah*. The *Matla'ul Anwar*, like its predecessor, is a book of moral precepts illustrated with anecdotes. The remaining four—*Shirin Khusrau, Majnun Laila, Aina-i Sikandari*, and *Hasht Bihisht*—deal with the same legends as Nizami. Khusrau certainly brought considerable powers to his task. His pen was as fluent as Nizami's and he composed with a marvellous rapidity; nor was he behind his predecessor in his knowledge of life and delicacy of feeling. Success was, nevertheless, out of the question. "Do not attempt to succeed in this art," says a well-known Persian line, "for it has reached its perfection in Nizami's hands." In the first place, Khusrau could never attain to the exuberant vigour and artistic fineness of Nizami's descriptive verse; again and again he essayed the task, and again and again he failed. But if Khusrau could not give us Nizami's scenes, he might have, as a compensation, told us better tales. But this was rendered impossible by the conditions Khusrau had imposed upon himself. He was going to write on the same four legends as Nizami. There were only two alternatives: he could repeat in his own words the stories Nizami had told before, but this would have been absurd; so Khusrau resorted to the plan of putting into verse the stories and incidents which Nizami had examined and thrown aside as incapable of artistic rendering. To this defect in his work Khusrau was quite alive. "The genius of Ganja," he says in his *Aina-i Sikandari*,(11) which fell flat by the side of its immortal predecessor, "was gifted with remarkable creative and critical faculties. When he took up this goblet—the tradition of Alexander, the Great—he carefully poured out all the clear wine for himself and only left the dregs for those who were to come after him. Carefully he weighed in the balance all that has been bequeathed to us by the wisdom of the ancients; he ignored such stories as were incapable of a poetic interpretation, and with the best he adorned his volume and secured for it a great popularity and reception wherever it went. (In this he was well-advised.) Versifying a worthless story is like writing abuses with musk; negroes who attempt to whiten their faces

---

(11) Aligarh edition, pages 25-28. I have translated only the more important lines of the passage.

only bring a smile to the lips of the wise. But since all the pearls have been carried away by my predecessor, I have no alternative but to string potsherds together; and if you object to my doing so, please blame the person who has put me to this task............ When the farmer takes away all corn from the field, the poor ant has to live on grains of earth. Nizami has left no good wine in the goblet, and none will flow out howsoever I may tilt it."

Contemporary critics did not fail to point out the deficiencies of Khusrau's works as they came out in rapid succession; and among them one, Obaid, surnamed 'the Poet,' a close friend of Sultan Mohammad bin Tughlaq, is credited with having remarked that it was "an irreverent presumption on Khusrau's part to boil his meat and rice in Nizami's cauldron." The *Khamsah* was the product of a life almost exclusively dedicated to it, and Khusrau's plan of writing something equal to it in the intervals of other business was foredoomed to failure. But he turned fiercely on his critics. "My *Majnun Laila* may not be equal to Nizami's work," he says with the *argumentum ad hominem* so familiar to logicians, "but it is not for every silly ass to estimate my worth. If I am devoid of art, will you not, on your part, undertake to produce something to enable me to judge of your powers? But your own work being worthless, you console yourself by singing Nizami's praise. You say his words bring the dead to life. Of course! But what are your own productions worth? Maybe, by flogging your dull mind you will succeed in composing some fifty or hundred verses in his style, but your lame horse will never go cantering and galloping *farsang* after *farsang*."(12)

He had, however, learnt to respect Nizami, and, in a passage remarkable for its sobriety and good sense, he does justice to Nizami and to his own work as well. "My ambitious heart had longed to reconstruct Nizami's magic, to cast a spell like his, so that I might claim that I could march to his measured steps. But I am now convinced of my shortcomings and acknowledge his pre-eminence. It is impossible to improve upon, or rival, the master's work, though I may claim in self-defence that it was impossible, sword in hand, to conquer the kingdom of another with greater success............ I have composed this *masnavi* (*Majnun Laila*) in order to awaken the people of these days; the sentiment that inspires it is the same as of its well-known predecessor. The reputation of my master lives for ever—if not, I shall bring him to life again. The great poet is worthy of praise. He has collected all that was excellent in his songs without leaving anything for me. But I, too, deserve commendation for having constructed my *masnavi* out of the stuff discarded by him. Nizami confined himself to a single branch of poetry; instead of frittering away his energy in all directions, he strove in the *masnavi* alone. He was a man of one art; so in that art he excelled the whole world. Surely, a man of discrimination will apply himself only to the work for which he has an aptitude! And to his one task the poet of

(12) *Majnun Laila,* Aligarh edition, page 169.

Ganja dedicated his whole life. He said 'good-bye' to the world and its attractions, and retreated to a quiet corner. His *masnavi* was the only demand on his time, the only burden on his heart. A secluded life, a mind unruffled by distracting cares, his livelihood provided by the generosity of princes and great men—how could a combination of such happy elements fail to produce poetry of the higest excellence? But I, unhappy man, boil with my worries like a cauldron. From morn to night and from night to morn I have never a moment of peace; my unbridled worldly ambition compels me to stand with folded hands before a patron no better than myself; and nothing comes into my hands till I have sweated in labour from head to foot. The payment made to me, moreover, is regarded as a gift, not a remuneration for my toil—like the ass which, after having carried its load, has its rationed grass thrown before its face with contempt. If, under these circumstances, I can find a week or sc of leisure, am I to devote it to praising my kindly patron or to expressing the poetic aspirations of my soul? And what sort of precious stones can one dig out of the rocks in such a short time? My good fortune consists in the fluency of my pen; I have only to tap my head and ideas come bubbling forth, while my verses are composed with a rapidity that leaves my thoughts behind. I have managed to write all this, in spite of innumerable distractions. Were the arduous task of earning a livelihood to leave me more leisure, I could show what I am capable of. In spite of all these drawbacks, a fair critic will acknowledge the talent displayed in my *Panj Ganj*: and if he does not, well, I am not ignorant of the value of my rubies."(13)

According to the general opinion of later critics, Khusrau has neither equalled nor surpassed Nizami, but he is, beyond doubt, the best of Nizami's many imitators. A man of his talents was sure to fare well in everything he undertook. But the plan of the *Panj Ganj* was unfortunate. Nizami had sucked all the blood out of the old Persian legends, and Khusrau would have been well-advised to explore a new field. The mythology of the Indians is as interesting and as capable of poetic interpretation as the traditional tales of the Persians; and the *Hasht Bihisht,* in which Khusrau allowed himself to incorporate a number of Indian stories, is the best of his romances. But the Mussalmans of his day had not discovered the poetry that lay enshrined in the *Ramayana* and the *Mahabharata;* Khusrau could not have forestalled Faizi any more than Alauddin could have forestalled Akbar; and the *Panj Ganj* is condemned by the staleness of its themes rather than the style of its story-telling. Nothing that was in Khusrau's power to write could have ever equalled the literary excellence of the *Khamsah;* but he could have told us different and better tales. Great respect has been, and always will be, paid to Khusrau and his *masnavis,* but not one of his ten volumes stands pre-eminent as a classic. They have always been revered but seldom

---

(13) *Majnun Laila,* Aligarh edition, pages 169-172

read. It was not by such slavish imitation that Nizami had improved upon the *Shah Namah.*

A few extracts in English may give the reader an idea of the sort of stories Khusrau tells, though not of the way in which he tells them:—

I. The Three Princes of Ceylon.

"Once upon a time there reigned in Ceylon a just and wise king, whose power was acknowledged up to the precincts of Ghaznin. He had three sons, who excelled in knowledge and learning as well as in bodily strength. One day the father, in order to discover if his sons had any designs against him, called the eldest Prince to a private interview and said: 'I have reached an advanced age and must retire to a corner and worship my God. You are the heir to the throne. Direct the affairs of the state with justice so that your subjects may be loyal and your God pleased. Be a good shepherd and do not leave your flock to the wolf.'

"The Prince placed his forehead on the ground. 'An ant may creep up to the throne, but it cannot become a Solomon,' he replied, 'I will not think of such a thing while Your Majesty is alive.'

"The king was pleased at heart with the heir-apparent's answer, but he pretended to be angry and drove him from his presence. Next he called his second son and offered the throne to him. But he also refused. 'It would be wrong of me,' he protested, 'to talk of the crown and the throne during Your Majesty's life. And when the passing of time has brought Your Majesty's happy reign to an end, it is my elder brother, not I, who will mount the throne. Small pearls are not fit ornaments for a crown.' The youngest brother, when called in his turn, gave a similar answer. Pleased though he was with their loyalty and affection, the king determined to test his sons still further and ordered them to leave the kingdom.

"The Princes were staggered by their father's order, but they loyally obeyed it; and, packing their belongings, they passed through cities and forests till they had crossed the frontier of the kingdom and were within the territory of another ruler. Now it happened that when the Princes were near the capital of this kingdom, an Ethiopian came running from the opposite direction. His face was black as tar. 'Gentle travellers!' he cried, 'Have you seen my camel?'

"'Had it lost one of its eyes?' asked the eldest Prince.

"'Had it lost one of its teeth?' asked the second.

"'Was it lame in one of its legs?' asked the third.

"'Since you have seen it,' cried the Ethiopian, 'tell me where to find it?'

"'Go straight and quick,' the three Princes replied simultaneously.

"The Ethiopian proceeded in search of his camel, while the Princes, after travelling some distance further, lay down to rest in the shade of a large tree. They were still at the spot when the Ethiopian returned, and complained in a voice sharp as the edge of a dagger: 'I have run a whole *farsang* over hill and plain, but I have not seen even the dust of my camel's feet.'

"'Hear us, brother,' replied the first Prince, 'It will not be right to conceal from you anything we know. Does your camel carry a jar of oil on one side of its back and a jar of honey on the other?'

"'And is not a woman seated on it also?' asked the second Prince.

"'And is not that woman in the last stage of pregnancy?' asked the third.

"These questions confirmed the Ethiopian's suspicion. He caught hold of the Princes and raised a cry that they were thieves, *thugs, badmashes,* who wandered up and down the country and stole the camels and property of honest people. A number of men collected together at the Ethiopian's cries, and, as was natural, all talked at the same time, so that none could be heard. After much altercation, however, it was decided to take the Princes to the king of the city for the punishment they were thought to deserve.

"When the case came up for trial, the Ethiopian related exactly all that had happened and the king asked the Princes to state their side of the case. 'May Your Majesty's reign be prolonged to the end of time!' replied the wisest of the Princes, 'We are three poor travellers whom an irrepressible longing to see the world has been driving over hill and plain. While we were coming towards Your Majesty's city, this black-faced Ethiopian ran up to us and insisted on our telling him the whereabouts of his camel; and we, on our part, by way of sport tried to make guesses about his camel in order to increase his anxiety.'

"The king was enraged. 'Not one guess in ten proves true,' he said, 'Give back what you have stolen, or prepare for the punishment you deserve.' And he sent the three Princes to prison, where they passed a miserable night in the company of thieves, robbers and cut-throats.

"Next morning a wood-cutter found the camel (with the woman on it) straying in the forest and brought it back to the Ethiopian, who immediately ran to inform the king. The king felt sorry for the miscarriage of justice and ordered the Princes to be released and brought before him.

"'Out with your secret!' he thundered, 'How did you know so much about the camel since you had never seen it? Tell me the whole truth, or I will cut off your heads.'

"The Princes bowed their foreheads to the ground. 'May Your Majesty be always happy and prosperous!' the eldest Prince replied, 'I discovered that the camel was half-blind by using my own eyes with care. As we walked towards the city, I saw that the leaves and branches on one side of the road had been eaten by the animal while those on the other side were left untouched.'

"'And I,' replied the second Prince, 'carefully studied the impressions left by the camel and saw clearly that it had been painfully dragging one of its legs.'

" 'On taking up some of the twigs and leaves left half-eaten by the camel,' added the third, 'I was left in no doubt that one of its teeth was missing.'

" 'That is good,' said the king, 'Now tell me what led you to make your other three remarks.'

" 'Drops of liquid had trickled down from the camel's back and fallen on the road,' the first Prince replied, 'On one side there was a swarm of flies and on the other a troop of ants. This could have only been due to honey and oil.'

" 'At one place it appeared from the impressions on the ground that the camel had squatted for a time,' the second Prince explained, 'And by the side of the marks left by the camel I saw the delicate impressions of a woman's shoes.'

" 'And, by the side of the footprints observed by my brother, I saw impressions of her hands also,' the third Prince added, 'The woman must be advanced in her pregnancy, I concluded, if she has to crawl on all fours in order to get on to the camel's back.'

" The king was mightily pleased at the intelligence displayed by the Princes. He presented them with robes of honour and gave them a house within the palace compound to live in. Often when the affairs of the state left him some leisure, he dropped in to chat with the Princes and marvelled at their wisdom and power of observation.

"Now one evening the king happened to send the Princes a present of roast lamb and wine, and the three brothers sat down to partake of it.

"'This wine seems to have a mixture of human blood in it,' remarked one of the Princes.

"'Nor is the flesh of this lamb pure,' said the second, 'It seems to have been nourished on the milk of a bitch.'

"'Why complain of these trifles,' added the third, 'when our king himself is not the real son of his predecessor. He has a butler's blood in his veins.'

"Meanwhile the king, who had hidden himself in an adjoining room, writhed like a snake at these remarks; and, quite unable to control himself any longer, he entered the chamber of the Princes. They respectfully rose up to receive him.

"'Speak out before me what you have been telling each other just now,' he ordered. The Princes, finding that they had been overheard, sought safety in truth. The king kept on drinking while they repeated their previous remarks. He was boiling with rage. But he knew them to be shrewd and intelligent, and though he said nothing at the time, he made a diligent inquiry into the truth of their assertions.

"The keeper of the royal cellars confessed that he had obtained his grapes from a vineyard, which had once been a graveyard.

"This discovery weighed heavily on the king's mind, and he became anxious lest the other remarks of the Princes should also turn out to be true. He called for the shepherd who had sold the lamb to the royal kitchen. The fellow swore emphatically that the lamb had been brought up on its own mother's milk, but the king refused to believe him. 'Out with the truth!' he shouted, 'or I will cut off your head like a blade of grass.' Finding at last that his only chance of escape lay in confessing the truth, the shepherd admitted that one of his lambs having been carried off by a wolf, he had hit upon the novel design of getting the motherless kid suckled by a bitch. 'She was a fine dog,' he explained, 'She flew like an arrow, and it was with great difficulty that I induced her to give suck to the kid along with her own puppies.'

"The most perplexing problem still remained. The king was seized with a sort of fever and would not rest till he had discovered everything. He hastened to his mother's chamber and asked her in a tone of extreme rudeness: 'Who is my real father—the late king or some one else? Tell me the bitter truth.'

"The queen-mother was shocked and surprised by her son's question. 'What is the matter with you,' she asked, 'that you put such questions to your own mother? Who but the king could have touched me? You ought to feel ashamed of yourself.'

"But her son refused to be put off like this and cast at his mother a look of bitter hatred and contempt. 'Nothing but the truth,' he said, 'will save you from the punishment your sins deserve.'

"The cowardly mother knew her son to be capable of *every* act of justice and at last confessed in a trembling voice: 'For years I have kept my secret undisclosed, but you shall hear my story, if your ears can stand the shock. It was the season of the spring. The king had gone out hunting. I had been sleeping alone in my chamber, when on opening my eyes I saw a butler enter the door with my food on a tray. I was young, in the vigour of my health and the blossom of my beauty; inspired by a passion that vanquished my self-control, I flew at him like one drunk and would not let him go till he had done my bidding. From that union you, my son, were born. It had been so inscribed in the book of my fate.'

" The king hung his head low at this confession of his mother's shame; and, bitterly regretting the question he had asked, dragged himself away from her chamber more dead than alive.

" In the evening he visited the house of the Princes, and, after a few rounds of the wine-cup, he addressed them thus: 'I have inquired into the assertions you made last night. All of them are perfectly true. But do tell me how you managed to discover these secrets.'

" 'I began to feel sad and gloomy the moment I tasted your wine last night,' the first Prince replied, 'and on inquiring from others I found that it had the same effect on them also. The natural effect of wine is to bring hilarity and joy, I argued; the grape, from which this wine has been made, must have drawn its nourishment from the blood and body of the dead.'

" 'As soon as I had put a morsel of the roast-mutton into my mouth,' replied the second Prince, 'my heart began to burn and palpitate and my mouth was filled with saliva. The mutton, moreover, smelt like the blood of fleas. This is the flesh of a dog, I concluded, or of a lamb brought up on the milk of a bitch.'

"'I, too, will speak out my mind if I am promised forgiveness,' the third Prince pleaded. The king assured him on a thousand oaths that his life and liberty were in no danger.

"'I have carefully observed all acts of Your Majesty ever since I have been at the court; and though I found them inspired by experience and wisdom, I failed to discover in them any of the traits which distinguish princes of royal blood. What particularly attracted my attention was the fact that Your Majesty seldom used a sentence in which there was no reference to bread and gravy. This enabled me to trace Your Majesty's descent to a butler.'

"The king kept silent for a moment after these disclosures. 'I must avoid shedding innocent blood,' he thought within himself, 'It would be best to send off my guests before my anger gets the better of my sense of justice.' Then turning towards the Princes he forced himself into a cheerful laugh. 'I congratulate you on your remarkable intelligence,' he said, 'But it would be cruel to keep birds of passage like you pent up within the walls of a single city.' And with many such apologies, and a present of a hundred gold pieces to each Prince, he bade them a cordial farewell.

"The three Princes returned to the kingdom of their father."

II. The Death of Majnun.

"The narrator of this ancient story will now explain how Laila, when dead, carried her lover with her.

"Laila's mother wept bitterly when she realised that her daughter was no more. She tore her hair and they were strewn about like camphor-flowers on her daughter's corpse. Friends and relations also collected together with their weeping eyes. Among them Majnun, who had heard of her illness, came to their house in a state of utter dejection to inquire how she was doing. He heard the sounds of wailing in the house, and immediately afterwards the funeral, followed by a procession of mourners, issued out of the door and began to move slowly through the streets.

"The sight of the funeral transformed Majnun all of a sudden. He rushed forward and walked before the funeral in a condition of ecstatic joy, dancing and singing. The gladness of his heart found vent in extempore and joyous verse. 'God be praised for the day on which I have been freed from the torture of separation and blessed with a union so close that there is no place for body or life between us! I have found my salvation without being obliged to others and revel in my love without fear of criticism. We will lie in the same chamber, face to face, sleep in the same bed, arm in arm. And from that sleep, which the sound of human voices cannot disturb, I will not raise my head till the Day of Resurrection. The pure soul will fly away with the pure soul; the dust will mingle with the dust. Do make our grave as small as possible, so that our bodies may be squeezed together; nor need I fear the closeness of the grave, for the garden of immortality is extensive enough............'

"Some there were who could understand the purport of Majnun's song; others smiled at his madness even in their tears, but they thought he was insane, and consequently took no serious notice of his actions.

"When the procession reached the graveyard, the corpse was laid in the newly dug grave, and the mourners were preparing to close it for ever. At that instant Majnun rushed out of the crowd and jumped into the grave; he lifted up the corpse and was seen pressing it against his face and bosom. This was too much for the relatives of the deceased girl. One or two of them jumped into the grave with drawn daggers to punish the desecrator for his crime. They twisted his neck and drew his lips away from the lips of the corpse; his vacant eyes looked at them with a cold, lifeless stare. They shook him; there was no sign of life in his limbs. His body had joined for ever the body of his beloved; his soul had flown away with her. And the arm he had wound round her waist refused to straighten.

"They wished to separate the two dead bodies but some old and experienced men present warned them against it. 'This is a symbol of divine mystery,' they said with their weeping eyes, 'and not a human passion, for who would give up his life for the sake of a mere desire? They retained their self-control in life; and in death their purity is clear to all. Be the responsibility of it on our heads, but do not separate in death those whose souls love had joined together.'

"So they closed the grave above the two lovers and returned weeping to their homes."

III. The Hindu and Muslim Pilgrims.

"A Muslim *haji* proceeding to Mecca met a Brahman pilgrim going to Somnath. Owing to the strength of his devotion, the Brahman was measuring the ground with his body and the stones of the road had torn off the skin of his breast. 'Whereto, friend?' the *haji* inquired. 'I have been travelling like this for several years,' the Brahman replied. 'But God has given you your two feet; why do you crawl on your breast instead of walking upon them?' 'Ever since I have dedicated my life to my idol, I crawl towards him on my breast and my heart,' the Brahman replied.

"And you, who laugh at the Hindus for being idolators, at least condescend to take a lesson from the sincerity of their faith. Granted, the arrow of the idolator is shot at a wrong target; but towards that target it is moving *straight*. How much more pathetic the condition of one who, knowing the true object of life, none the less shoots in a wrong direction! Go on thy path like a straight arrow, O my master, so that they may rightly call thee the warrior of the Lord."

Khusrau's poetical genius was not descriptive but lyric. It is in his *ghazals* that we see him at his best and it is by his *ghazals* that he is chiefly remembered. The invention of this form of verse is ascribed to Shaikh Sa'di of Shiraz, whose wandering, insecure life had made him familiar with every variety of human emotion. Khusrau imitated Sa'di in the *ghazal* as he had imitated Nizami in the *masnavi*, but this time there was no slavishness in his imitation. His four ponderous *Diwans—Tuhfatus Sighar, Wastul Hayat, Gharratul Kamal* and *Baqiah Naqiah*—have, no doubt, many defects. Their volume is too great a burden on the shoulders of posterity.(16) He composed too rapidly and too carelessly, and as most of the *ghazals* were written not from 'the fulness of

---

(14) "The first *Diwan* of Amir Khusrau is the *Tuhftatus Sighar* (The Present of Youth), containing the poems which he wrote from the 16th to the 19th year of his age. These were written in the time of Sultan Balban, and contain several panegyrics addressed to him. In compliment to his sovereign title, he here frequently assumes to himself the poetical designation of *Sultani.* Most of the *qasidas* in this *Diwan,* which are not devoted to the Sultan, were written in celebration of new year festivals and *Ids,* or addressed to the king's eldest son, Nusratuddin Sultan Mohammad Khan, known better as the *Khan-i Shahid,* or the 'Martyr Prince,' and to contemporary ministers and nobles. The *tarjis* are addressed to the author's spiritual teacher, Nizamuddin Aulia, Sultan Balban, and his son above named. It includes also a poem in praise of Malik Ikhtiaruddin, the *Ariz.*

"The second *Diwan* is the *Wastul Hayat* (The Middle of Life), containing the poems written from the 24th to the 32nd year of his life. These are in praise chiefly of Nizamuddin Aulia, and the prince above named, then governor of the Punjab and Multan, who was slain in an action with the Mongols at Dipalpur, at the close of the year 683 A.H. The poet was in his service. One panegyric is addressed to Sultan Muizuddin Kai-Kabad, and another to Ikhtiaruddoulah Chajju Khan-i Muazzam, the son of Kishlu Khan, nephew of Sultan Balban, and governor of Karra-Manikpur. Others are

the heart but the emptiness of the pocket,' an endless repetition of the same ideas and phrases could hardly be avoided. Three-fourths of the mass, at least, is pure hack-work, a useless versification of commonplace ideas. For this Khusrau is not to blame. His princely patrons wanted a basketful of *ghazals* every day and the poet was compelled to provide the fare. But as the reader traverses page after page, some of the *ghazals* shine out brilliantly from the dull mass; they are the poet's genuine and inspired work; and

---

addressed to the *Ariz,* Tajuddin, Fathul Mulk Sharfuddin, Alp Khan Ghazi, son of Azhdar Malik, Naib Shah Malik Ikhtiaruddin Ali bin Aibak, and other nobles.

"The third *Diwan* is the *Gharratul Kamal* (Perfect Light), containing poems written from the 34th to the 42nd year of his life. It opens with an intere ng preface, containing some autobiographical notices. These poems comprise panegyrics upon Nizamuddin Aulia, Sultan Kai-Kabad, Shayista Khan, who for a short time ruled the state in the name of Shamsuddin, the son of Kai-Kabad, and afterwards became king under the title of Jalaluddin, Sultan Ruknuddin Ibrahim, youngest son of Jalaluddin, who sat for a short time on the throne of Delhi after the murder of his father, Sultan Alauddin, Ikhtiaruddin Ali bin Aibak, Saifuddoulah Barbak, Tajuddin, Alp Khan Ghazi, and Tajuddoulah Malik Chajju; an elegy upon the death of Khan-i Khanan Mahmud, Sultan Ikhtiaruddin, the son of Jalaluddin, and benedictions addressed to his other sons, Khan-i Muazzam Arkalah Khan and Khan-i Azam Qadr Khan. This *Diwan* contains also odes on new year festivals and the *Ids,* and, besides the *masnavis* mentioned above, the poet addresses one to his brother, Zahid Khan, descriptive of his accompanying the royal army in 687 A.H. to Oudh. Another is in praise of the palace at Kilukhari and of its founder, Sultan Kai-Kabad. Size of the work, 4to., 694 pages of an average of 15 lines.

"The fourth *Diwan* is called the *Baqiah Naqiah* (The Pure Remnant), containing poems written by Amir Khusrau from the 50th to the 64th year of his age. There are in it panegyrics on Nizammuddin Aulia, Shaikh Alauddin, grandson of Shaikh Fariduddin Ganj-i Shakar, Sultan Alauddin, Sultan Kutubuddin Mubarakshah Shamsul Haq Khizr Khan,

Khusrau would have been well-advised to pick up the pearls and throw off the shells as Ghalib and Virgil have done. Unfortunately, he adopted the opposite course, edited all his *ghazals* according to the period of his life at which they were written, and with a kind cruelty to himself, his biographers and his critics, insisted on the preservation of every line. But even the educated public has refused to read his *Diwans* and knows him only through 'selections.'

As a writer of *ghazals* Khusrau has been equalled but not surpassed. His mind held in a happy proportion the two elements required to produce lyric poetry of the highest excellence—a fine ear for music and a heart that feels and can express its feelings. He began as a young gallant and ended as a mystic. He knew women, and the feelings that women inspire, but his horizon was not confined to that world alone. There is a sweetness in his words—a harmony and

---

eldest son of Sultan Alauddin, Nasirul Mulk Haji, Hamiddoulah, Tajuddoulah, Fakhruddin Pulad Tughlik, Muizzul Haq, Azam Alp Khan, Malik Ikhtiyaruddin Sadi, Malik Hisamuddin Khan-i Azam and Nasiruddin. There is an elegy on the Sultan's death on the 8th of Shawwal, 715 A.H., and some *masnavis* on the marriage of the princes and other matter." (*Elliot & Dowson,* Vol. II, pages 534-536.)

Some forty manuscripts of Khusrau's work are to be found in the India Office Library. The four *Diwans* I have examined are beautifully written and almost complete. The *ghazals* are written in the centre of the page and the *masnavis* on the margin. The prose introductions are in Khusrau's usual style. The *Diwans* have not yet been printed. Manuscript selections of Khusrau's *ghazals* were abundant in the middle ages and testify to his popularity; and one often comes across them even now. One such manuscript has been printed by the Newal Kishore Press, Lucknow, but the selection seems to have been indiscriminately made.

flow in the mere sound of them—that is found in Hafiz but, perhaps, not in any other Persian poet. If there was not a shred of sense and meaning in the words of Khusrau's finest lines, their rhythm and sound alone would suffice to make them immortal. He is the favourite poet of the mystic singers (*qawwals*) who have loved to set his lines to music, and advanced mystics have often fainted and yielded up the ghost at their recitation. In him, for the first (though not for the last) time, Persian poetry reaches its high-water mark—the sustained *ghazal.*

Translation will give no idea of the rhythm and beauty of the original:—

I (15)

O thou, beyond all comprehension
How can my thoughts e'er reach to Thee?
Or my vain intellect understand
Thy attribute or quality?

And over the great creation stands
The spaceless *pillar of Thy might.*
My soul, a feeble, wingless bird,
How shall it climb that endless height?

A thousand martyrs like Hussain
Have perished in the endless strife,
Yet human lips have never touched
Thy water of eternal life.

(15) *Kulliyat,* published by Newal Kishore Press: *Ai zi khiyal ma birun bar tu khiyal kai rasad.*

And day and night Thy light doth shine
Upon the throne of human heart,
Although our intellect never can
Thy vision to our eyes impart.

To earnest, humble pilgrims come
The words of mercy from Thy seat;
Khusrau, to idol-worship given,
Can but Thy outward symbols greet.

II (16)

Pleasant the grove, pleasant the fields,
Pleasant the advent of the spring!
Pleasant beneath a poplar tree
To hear above the bulbul *sing,*
To pass the cup from hand to hand
While music in our ears doth ring!

Fly, Zephyr, nimbly to her side
And softly with this message greet:
"Pleasant the lawn, pleasant the dew,
Pleasant the running water sweet!"
And bring her quickly to my arms
That in soft love our lips may meet.

'Tis pleasant with wine-heated blood
To kiss, to caress and cajole:
From her the wantonness of youth,
The cry of pain from Khusrau's soul.

---

(16) *Qiranus Sa'dain*, Aligarh edition, page 72: *Amad bahar o shud chaman o lalah-zar khush.*

III (17)

Thou takest life out of our clay
And yet within our hearts doth live—
Inflicting on us pang on pang
Doth yet a palliative give.

Thy flashing sword has laid all waste
The troubled garden of my heart;
Yet what a glory to this wreck
The rays of Thy great throne impart!

" The two vain, empty worlds," they say,
" Is price that all must pay for Thee."
Raise up the value, raise the cost.
This is too cheap—as all can see.

From this vain tenement of clay
My soul one day shall freedom find;
And yet my heart for ever shall
Remain with Thy great love entwined.

Khusrau! Thy grey locks and old age
Sort not with love for idols young!
And yet for such a senseless quest
Thou hast thy soul for ever flung.

---

(17) *Kulliyat,* Newal Kishore Press edition, page 275: *Jan za tan burdi wa dar jani hanauz.*

CHAPTER III

PROSE WORKS

Poetry was Amir Khusrau's mother tongue; prose he wrote with difficulty and effort, and he would have been well-advised to leave that region of literature to more pedestrain intellects. But such considerations could not check his exuberant genius. Apart from the introductions to his *Diwans,* two of his prose works, differing in volume and value, have survived to us. The first, *'Ijaz-i Khusravi* (Miracles of Khusrau) is a long work in five volumes on figures of speech.(1) It treats of every variety of 'miracle' known to the writers of the age—petitions to high officers composed of vowels only, verses which are Persian if read from right to left and Arabic if read from left to right, compositions from which all letters with dots are excluded, and many such *tours de force* which may have delighted and consoled the author's contemporaries but make no appeal to modern taste. Some of the letters included in the volumes have a solid historical value. An application to a government officer requesting for a post or complaining against the misbehaviour of neighbours was sure to

---

(1) Published, with marginal explanations, by the Newal Kishore Press, Lucknow.

attract attention if drafted by Khusrau; and the poet was too inventive not to have a new 'miracle' ready for every occasion. It is easy to understand that supplicants flocked to his door.(2) He seems also to have beguiled his leisure hours in discovering new literary tricks and often sent them as presents to his friends. The *'Ijaz-i Khusravi* is the accumulated mass of these miraculous prose compositions, which Amir Khusrau had been amassing for years and edited in the later part of Alauddin's reign. Most of the pieces are tiresome and frivolous, but others throw a brilliant light on the social life of the day. Amir Khusrau's second prose work, the *Khazainul Futuh,* is the official history of Alauddin's campaigns.

Amir Khusrau was a man of wit and humour. His fancies are often brilliant. Nevertheless, nothing but a stern sense of duty will induce a modern reader to go through Khusrau's prose works in the original. His style is artificial in the extreme; the similes and metaphors are sometimes too puerile even for a schoolboy; at other places the connecting link between the ideas (if present at all) is hard to discover. Prose is the natural speech of man for ordinary occasions, but Amir Khusrau's ideas seem to have come to him in a versified form. So, while his poetry has all the beauties of excellent prose, his prose has all the artificiality of very bad verse; it is jejune, insipid, tasteless and wearisome. Failing to realise that the true beauty of prose lies in its being simple, direct and

---

(2) One of the letters has been translated in *Elliot & Dowson.* There are others of equal (or greater) value.

effective, he tries to surprise his readers by a new trick at every turn, attacks him with words the meaning of which he is not likely to know, or offers him metaphors and similes calculated to shock and disgust. His one desire is to convince the reader of his own mental powers and in this, so far as contemporaries were concerned, he certainly succeeded. But Amir Khusrau, for all his artistic talent, never comprehended that a book of prose, like a volume of verse, should be a thing of beauty and of joy.

The *Khazainul Futuh* very well illustrates the general character of Khusrau's prose. It is divided into small paragraphs; every paragraph has a heading informing the reader what allusions he is going to find in the next few lines. A single example will suffice.

Allusions to Water.

"If the *stream* of my life was given the boon of *eternal existence,* even then I would not offer the *thirsty* any *drink* except the praises of the Second Alexander.(3) But as I find that human life is such that in the end we have to *wash* our hands off it, the *fountain* of words will only enable the reader to *moisten* his lips. Since the achievement of my life, from the cradle to the grave, cannot be more than this, I did not think it proper to *plunge* to the bottom of endless *oceans,* but contented myself with a small quantity of the *water of life.*"

And so it goes on, wearisome and artificial, from beginning to end.

---

(3) Alluding to the first Alexander's efforts to discover the water of immortality.

It is obvious that such a procedure detracts much from the value of an historical work. Only such facts can be stated as will permit Khusrau to bring in the requisite allusion; the rest will be only partially stated or ignored. Khusrau's only resource was to make his paragraphs as small as possible; otherwise his prose would have marched along routes quite different from those selected by Alauddin's generals. The reader, who wishes to discover the true historical fact, has first to solve Khusrau's literary conundrums and then critically separate the element of fact from the colouring imparted to it by Khusrau in order to bring in the allusions. At times the literary trick makes us ignore the fact at the bottom.

Allusions to Virtue and Vice.

"Though the giving of water (to the thirsty) is one of the most notable *virtues* of this *pure-minded* Emperor, yet he has removed wine with all its *accompaniments* from *vicious* assemblies; for *wine*, the daughter of grape and the sister of sugar, is the *mother of all wickedness.* And wine, on her part, has washed herself with salt, and sworn that she will henceforth remain in the form of vinegar, freeing herself from all *evils* out of regard for the *claims of salt.*"(4)

This would have appeared a mere literary flourish if we had not been definitely told by Ziauddin Barni that Alauddin carried through a series of harsh measures for the suppression of drinking in Delhi.

---

(4) Wine and sugar may be both produced from the same grapes, and the addition of salt turns wine into vinegar.

Conversely, the allusion may have no basis of fact at all.

Allusions to Sea and Rain.

"The sword of the righteous monarch completely conquered the province (Gujerat). Much *blood* was *shed*. A general invitation was issued to all the beasts and birds of the forest to a continuous feast of meat and drink. In the marriage banquet, at which the Hindus were sacrificed, animals of all kinds ate them to their satisfaction."

This would seem to indicate a general and intentional massacre. But there was no such massacre, and Khusrau himself goes on to assure us: "My object in this simile is not real blood, but (only to show) that the sword of Islam purified the land as the sun purifies the earth." The *Khazainul Futuh* has to be interpreted with care, and in the light of other contemporary material; it would be dangerous and misleading to accept Khusrau's accounts at their face value. Still, the labour of interpretation is well repaid by the new facts we discover.

The *Khazainul Futuh* naturally falls into six parts—(1) the introduction, (2) administrative reforms and public works, (3) campaigns against the Mongols, (4) the campaigns in Hindustan, (5) the campaign of Warangal and (6) the campaign of Ma'bar. The space devoted to the various sections is unequal. About two-thirds of the book is devoted to the Warangal and Ma'bar campaigns, while the other measures of Alauddin's reign are summarised in the remaining third. The reason for this is, perhaps, not impossible to discover. A remark of Barni [5] seems to throw light on the real character of the *Khazainul Futuh* as well as the *Tarikh-i Ferozi.* "The other great historian of the time (of Alauddin) was Kabiruddin, son of Tajuddin Iraqi. In the art of composition and eloquence he surpassed his contemporaries, and became the *amir-i dad-i lashkar* in place of his revered father. He was held in great honour by Alauddin. He has displayed wonders in Arabic and Persian prose. In the *Fath-i Namah* (Book of Victory), which consists of several volumes, he does honour to the traditions of prose and seems to surpass all writers, ancient and modern. But of all the events of Alauddin's reign, he has confined himself to a narration of the Sultan's conquests; these he has praised with exaggeration and adorned with figures of speech, and he has departed from the tradition of those historians, who relate the good as well as the bad actions of every man. But as he wrote the history of Alauddin during that Sultan's reign and every volume of it was presented to the Sultan, it was impossible for him to refrain from praising that terrible king or to speak of anything but his greatness."

So Amir Khusrau, though the poet-laureate, was not the court-historian of Alauddin Khilji; that honour belonged to Kabiruddin, who was considered to be the greatest prose writer of the day. The official history, through which Alauddin expected to be remembered by posterity, was not the thin volume of Amir Khusrau but the ponderous *Fath-i Namah,* which was prepared

---

(5) *Tarikh-i Ferozi,* page 361.

under the Sultan's personal supervision. The *Fath-i Namah* has disappeared; its manuscripts may have been intentionally destroyed during Timur's invasion or under the early Moghul Emperors, for it must have been full of contempt and hatred towards the Mongol barbarians (6); Ferishta and other later historians do not refer to it; its great length would, in any case, have made its preservation difficult. But Barni and Khusrau had the *Fath-i Namah* before them and accommodated their histories to it. Barni, who was essentially a man of civil life, allowed Kabiruddin to speak of Alauddin's conquests and confined his own history to an account of administrative and political affairs, merely adding a paragraph on the campaigns here and there for the logical completeness of his work. Amir Khusrau was more ambitious. He pitted himself against Kabiruddin's great, if transient, reputation and on Kabiruddin's own chosen ground. Hitherto his pen, "like a tire-woman, had generally curled the hair of her maidens in verse," but it would now bring "pages of prose for the high festival." Let not critics dismiss him as a mere poet, living in a mock paradise and incapable of describing the affairs of government and war. If he had wings to fly, he had also feet to walk. He would even surpass Kabiruddin, whom shallow critics considered 'the greatest of all prosaists, ancient and modern.' He would excel

(6) The same fate has overtaken other mediæval histories, for example, the first volume of *Baihaqi*, the *Autobiography of Mohammad bin Tughlaq* and the last chapter of Afif's *Tarikh-i Feroz Shahi,* which was a violent attack on Timur and is found torn or missing in most volumes.

wherever Kabiruddin had excelled. The four virtues (or defects) which Barni deploringly attributes to Kabiruddin are all painfully present in Khusrau's work—an artificial style adorned with figures of speech, an exclusive devotion to wars and conquests, the elimination of all facts that were not complimentary to Alauddin, and, lastly, an exaggerated flattery of the Sultan. In the *Panj Ganj*, he had imitated the *Khamsah* of Nizami and walked, as far as possible, in his predecessor's footsteps. It was a mistake, but he repeated it once more in the *Khazainul Futuh*. We do not see Khusrau's prose in its natural dress; it is draped and disfigured into an imitation of Kabiruddin's extinct composition. For Amir Khusrau, if a scholar, was also courtier, and the courtier is a devotee to the fashion of the passing hour. The fashion had been set by Kabiruddin and his predecessors. Khusrau blindly followed it.

The *Khazainul Futuh* is not merely a challenge to the *Fath-i Namah* of Kabiruddin; it is also a continuation of it. Barni seems to imply that Kabiruddin was a survivor from the preceding age and he may not have lived to complete his voluminous work. If so, the disproportionate length of the Deccan campaigns in the *Khazainul Futuh* becomes intelligible. It is essentially a history of the Deccan invasions. Alauddin may have asked Khusrau to continue Kabiruddin's work, but Khusrau's introductory remarks make it probable that he wrote on his own initiative and expected the Sultan to accept it as the official account of the reign. The *Fath-i Namah* had made a detailed description of the earlier events unnecessary, and Khusrau merely summarises them to enable his book to stand on its own feet. But the Deccan campaigns are given in detail, probably after the manner of the extinct *Fath-i Namah.*

Amir Khusrau wished his work to be an official account of Alauddin's reign and the *Khazainul Futuh* has, consequently, all the merits and defects of a government publication. It credits Alauddin with every variety of virtue and power, and his officers also come in for their share. All governments live on lies, or, at least, a partial suppression of truth. But Amir Khusrau's hyperbolic exaggerations were less deceptive and dangerous than the insidious propaganda of modern governments. His exaggerated flattery neither deceived nor was intended to deceive; it was simply a current fashion and nobody attached any significance to the words used. Exaggeration is not a commendable habit; but understand it as a habit, and it will no longer veil the true meaning of the author.

Ziauddin Barni complains that Kabiruddin simply confined himself to those events which were creditable to Alauddin. This is certainly true of Khusrau's work. He will not utter a lie, but neither will he speak 'the truth and the whole truth.' On the 16th Ramzan, 695 A.H. (July 9, 1296 A.D.) Sultan Jalaluddin was assassinated on the bank of the Ganges by the order of Alauddin Khilji, who was then governor of Karra. It was an atrocious murder, but Amir Khusrau simply ignores it. "As Providence had ordained that this Muslim Moses was to seize the powerful swords from all infidel Pharoahs..........he mounted the throne on Wednesday, 16th Ramzan, 695 A.H." What else was there to say? He was not brave enough to condemn the murder of his patron nor mean enough to praise it. He simply turned away his eyes. Similar omissions strike us in the chapter on the Mongols. Nothing is said of the campaigns in which Alauddin's armies were defeated. The Mongols twice besieged Delhi and Alauddin's position became extremely critical.(7) But Khusrau has not even indirectly alluded to these momentous events. We are able to make up for some of the omissions with the help of Barni and other historians, but we cannot be certain that all the gaps have been filled.

In spite of these serious shortcomings, the *Khazainul Futuh* is, for the critical student, a book of solid worth. Amir Khusrau exaggerates and we can make allowance for his exaggerations. He leaves blanks which other historians enable us to fill up. But he is too honest and straightforward to tell a lie, and we can safely rely on his word. He is exact in details and dates, and enables us to make a fairly complete chronology of Alauddin's reign.(8) In spite of the artificiality of his style, his descriptions have the vivid touches of an eye-witness. He is a soldier

---

(7) In the first invasion the Mongols were led by Kutlugh Khwaja and in the second by Targhi. Barni, who is brief and hasty in his accounts of wars, gives a detailed account of the two sieges of Delhi, probably because Kabiruddin and Amir Khusrau had preferred to be silent about them.

(8) Barni, our standard historian for the period, is very parsimonious and incorrect in dates.

at home in military affairs, in the construction of siege-engines and the tactics of the battle-field; and a careful examination of the *Khazainul Futuh* will enable us to obtain a fairly good idea of the art of war in the early middle ages. Even where he tells us nothing new, he serves to confirm the accounts of others. He did not sit and brood in a corner. He mingled with the highest and the greatest in the land, and when he took up his pen, it was to write with a first hand knowledge of affairs. His chapters on the Deccan campaigns are a permanent contribution to Indian historical literature. They embody the romance of a jingoistic militarism, no doubt, but a romance none the less—long and heroic marches across 'paths more uneven than a camel's back,' temples plundered, *Rajas* subdued and the hoarded wealth of centuries brought at a swoop to the terrible Sultan of Delhi. It was a mad dance of rapine, ambition and death. "The Hindu *rawats* came riding in troops but were laid low before the Turkish horses. A deluge of water and blood flowed forward in order to plead for mercy before the Caliph's troops. Or, you might say, that owing to the great happiness of the infidel souls the beverage of blood was so delicious, that every time the cloud rained water over it, the ferocious earth drank it up with the greatest avidity. But in spite of the great intoxicating power of this wine, the *saqi* poured her clear liquid out of the flagon of the sky to increase its intoxication further. Out of this wine and beverage Death had manufactured her first delicious draught. *Next you saw bones on the earth.*"

If Amir Khusrau had been writing in the age of the *Puranas,* he would have represented Alauddin as an incarnation of Vishnu and described his opponents as malicious demons. That is how the Aryans blackened the character of their enemies and justified their own aggression. A modern writer would whitewash the same cruelties by talking of liberty, justice, the duty of elevating backward races and, with solemn, unconscious humour, advance the most humane arguments to justify the inhumanities of war. But Amir Khusrau was not a hypocrite; he saw life through plain glasses and the traditions of his day made hypocrisy unnecessary. The Deccan expeditions had one clear object—the acquisition of horses, elephants, jewels, gold and silver. Why tell lies? The Mussalmans had not gone there on a religious mission; they had neither the time nor the inclination to enrol converts, and they were too good soldiers to allow an irrelevant consideration to disturb their military plans. Of anything like an idealistic, even a fanatic, religious mission the Deccan invasions were completely innocent. Of course the *name* of God was solemnly pronounced. The invaders built mosques wherever they went and the call to prayer resounded in many a wilderness and many a desolated town. It was their habit.

But it would be a serious mistake to interpret the political movements of those days in the light of modern national feeling or of the religious enthusiasm of the early Saracens. The fundamental social and political principle of the Middle Ages was loyalty to the salt. It overrode all racial, communal and religious considerations. The *Raja's* Muslim servants followed him against the Sultan, just as the Sultan's Hindu servants followed him against the *Raja*. Loyalty to the salt (*namak halali*) was synonymous with patriotism; disloyalty to the salt (*namak harami*) was a crime blacker than treason. Irrational as the principle may seem, it prevented communal friction and worked for peace. Conversely, for the ruler all his subjects stood on an equal footing. The Hindu subjects of a neighbouring *Raja* were the proper and inviting objects of 'a holy war,' but not the Sultan's own Hindu subjects. They were under his protection, and his prosperity depended on their prosperity. Learned writers may call them *zimmis* (payers of tribute) in books of religious law. But men of practical affairs knew the ground they stood on and the power of the mass of the people. The temples in the Sultan's dominions were perfectly safe. "It is not permissible to injure a temple of long standing," was the *fatwa* (judgment) of a *qazi* in the reign of Sikandar Lodi, and it undoubtedly expresses mediæval sentiment on the matter. The Sultan could prohibit the building of a new temple or mosque, though, apart from occasional vagaries, the right was rarely exercised; but the destruction of a standing temple is seldom, if ever, heard of. It was, however, different with a temple standing in the dominion of another ruler; it had no imperial guarantee to protect it and could be plundered with impunity because its devotees were not the Sultan's subjects and their disloyalty and sufferings could do him no harm. The outlook of the age was essentially secular. Religion was a war cry—and nothing more.

A superficial reader of the *Khazainul Futuh* would be inclined to think it inspired by bigotry and fanaticism. But this would be a serious error. Amir Khusrau's religious outlook was singularly tolerant: an examination of his *Diwans* can leave no other impression on the critic's mind. Even in the most bitter expressions of the *Khazainul Futuh,* there is a veiled suggestion. Of what? " So the temple of Somnath was made to bow towards the Holy Mecca, and as the temple lowered its head and jumped into the sea, you may say the building first said its prayers and then had a bath. The idols, who had fixed their abode midway to the House of Abraham (Mecca) and waylaid stragglers, were broken to pieces in pursuance of Abraham's tradition. But one idol, the greatest of them all, was sent by the *maliks* to the Imperial Court, so that the breaking of their helpless god may be demonstrated to the idol-worshipping Hindus." " They saw a building (the temple of Barmatpuri), old and strong as the infidelity of Satan and enchanting like the allurements of worldly life. You might say it was the Paradise of Shaddad, which, after being lost, those hellites had found, or that it was the golden Lanka of Ram............ The foundations of this golden temple, which was the 'holy place' of the Hindus, were dug up with the greatest care. The 'glorifiers of God' broke the infidel building, so that 'spiritual birds' descended on it like pigeons from the air. The 'ears' of the wall opened at the sound of the spade. At its call the sword also raised its head from the scabbard; and the heads of Brahmans and idol-worshippers came dancing from their trunks at the flashes of the sword. The golden bricks rolled down and brought with them their plaster of sandal-wood; the yellow gold became red with blood, and the white sandal turned scarlet. The sword flashed where the jewels had once been sparkling; where mire used to be created by rose-water and musk, there was now mud of blood and dirt; the saffron-coloured doors and walls assumed the colour of bronze; the stench of blood was emitted by ground once fragrant with musk. And at this smell the men of Faith were intoxicated and the men of Infidelity ruined."

Is this the trumpet of a bloated fanaticism or the excruciating melody of the tragic muse? Was Amir Khusrau praising the idol-breakers or bewailing their lack of true faith? It must not be forgotten that a courtier presenting an official history to the Sultan had no freedom of opinion, and Amir Khusrau emphatically expresses his willingness to recast his book according to the Sultan's wishes. But as Mohammad ibn-i Khawind Shah (Mirkhond), the author of *Rauzatus Safa,* remarks, the official historian should, by hints, insinuations, overpraise and such other devices as may come to hand, never fail to express his true opinion, which, while remaining undetected by his illiterate patron, cannot fail to be understood by the intelligent and the wise. Amir Khusrau had no liking for the *Malik Naib* Kafur-i Sultani, whom he abuses in the *Dawal Rani.* His keen sense of the religious and the poetic element in life could not but revolt against the senseless vandalism of the Deccan campaigns.

Hence the gruesome realism of his sketches. He may or may not have wept tears of blood over the fall of an ancient civilization; but his mode of expression leaves little doubt that the greed of gain, and not the service of the Lord, was the inspiring motive of the invaders. One thing alone was clear after the day of stormy battle: "*You saw bones on the earth.*"

FINIS